## Bits and Pieces

Cover and book design by Jonathan Kremer
Cover illustration by Sarah Lazarovic
Cartography by Karen Van Kerkoerle

Reinhartz, Henia, 1926 -
    Bits and pieces: memoirs / by Henia Reinhartz.
    (Azrieli Series of Holocaust Survivor Memoirs)

Includes bibliographical references and index.
ISBN 978-1-897470-00-8


1. Reinhartz, Henia, 1926 -. 2. Holocaust, Jewish (1939-1945)—Poland—Personal narratives. 3. Jewish children in the Holocaust—Poland—Biography. 4. Holocaust survivors—Canada—Biography. I. Azrieli Foundation. II. York University (Toronto, Ont.). Centre for Jewish Studies. III. Title. IV. Series.

D804.196.R44 2007     940.53'18092     C2007-905443-9

Printed in Canada

The Azrieli Foundation
164 Eglinton Avenue East
Suite 503
Toronto, Ontario
Canada M4P 1G4

Centre for Jewish Studies
York University
241 Vanier College
4700 Keele Street
Toronto Ontario
Canada M3J 1P3

# The AZRIELI SERIES of Holocaust Survivor Memoirs

Learn about other volumes in this series at: www.azrielifoundation.org

SERIES PREFACE

# In their own words...

The Azrieli Foundation – York University Holocaust Survivor Memoirs Publishing Program (Canada) was established to preserve and share the written memoirs of those who survived the twentieth century Nazi genocide of the Jews of Europe and who later made their way to Canada. The Program is guided by the conviction that each survivor of the Holocaust has a remarkable story to tell, and that such stories have an important role in education about tolerance and diversity.

Millions of individual stories are lost to us forever. The murdered Jews of Europe, of course, did not leave behind memoirs of their final days. By preserving the stories that survivors have written, and making them accessible to a broad public, the Program aims to sustain the memory of all those who perished at the hands of hatred, abetted by indifference and apathy. The personal accounts of those who survived against all odds are as different as the people who wrote them, but all demonstrate the courage, strength, wit and luck that it took to face and outlive terrible adversity. More than half a century later, the diversity of stories allows readers to put a face on what was lost, and to grasp the enormity of what happened to six million Jews — one story at a time. The memoirs are also moving tributes to people — strangers and friends — who risked their lives to help others, and who, through acts of kindness and decency in the darkest of moments, frequently helped the persecuted maintain faith in humanity and courage to endure. The accounts of how these survivors went on to build new lives in Canada after the war offers inspiration to all, as does their desire to share their experiences so that new generations can learn from them.

The Program seeks to collect, archive, edit and publish these distinctive historical records from fellow Canadians, and make them easily and freely accessible through Canadian libraries, Holocaust memorial organizations and online at The Azrieli Foundation website. The York University Centre for Jewish Studies has provided scholarly assistance and guidance in the editing and preparation of these memoirs for publication. The manuscripts as originally submitted are preserved in the Clara Thomas Archives and Special Collections at York University, and are available for review by interested scholars. These memoirs are published under the imprint The Azrieli Series of Holocaust Survivor Memoirs.

The Azrieli Foundation – York University Holocaust Survivor Memoirs Publishing Program gratefully acknowledges the many people who assisted in the preparation of this series for publication. Special thanks go to Jody Spiegel, Executive Coordinator of the Azrieli Foundation. For their invaluable contributions in editing, fact-checking and proof-reading the manuscripts, the Program is grateful to Todd Biderman, Helen Binik, Tali Boritz, Mark Celinscak, Mark Clamen, Jordana DeBloeme, Andrea Geddes-Poole, Valerie Hébert, Joe Hodes, Tomaz Jardim, Irena Kohn, Tatjana Lichtenstein, Carson Philips, Randall Schnoor, Tatyana Shestakov, and Mia Spiro. For their help and support in numerous ways, the Program would like to thank Susan Alper, Mary Arvanitakis, Howard Aster, Miriam Beckerman, François Blanc, Sheila Fischman, Esther Goldberg, Agripino Monteiro, Stan Morantz (Andora Graphics), Ariel Pulver, Michael Quddus, Henia Reinhartz, Nochem Reinhartz, Mark Veldhoven and Don Winkler.

All who are scattered like far-flung...
Together! Together! The flag is high,
Straining with anger, red with blood,
So swear together to live or die!

Earth with its heaven hear...
Bear witness, bright stars,
To our vow of blood and tear...
We swear. We swear. We swear.

We swear to strive for tr... m and right
Against the tyrant an... to be a force for...
... batt... ...rave, together...

W... ...stalwa... ...ists,
...th... rob and ...oor;
...Ts... ...masters, c... italis...
...venge... will be... ...ft and sure,
...ve or die!

...e vow,
...ong.
So swear together to live or die!

To the Bund, our hope and faith, we swear
Devotedly to set men free,
Its flag, bright scarlet, waves up there,
Sustaining us in loyalty.
So swear together to live or die!

# Bits and Pieces

*These are bits and pieces of my life.*

*They are for you, my little children, my grandchildren: Miriam-Simma, Mordkhele Avraham, Benjamin Abrasha, Shoshana Bryna, Leah Avrial and Simkha Ephraim Shimshon. Perhaps when you read this you will not be little any more, but for me you will always remain my little children.*

*Each one of you, my uniquely beautiful grandchildren, is my miracle and each of you has filled my life with riches that I cherish. I am putting down those bits and pieces for you because Ima and Daddy already know most of the stories of my life, and because I would like you also to know where I come from, who my parents were, what my world was like when I was growing up. I know how difficult it must be for you to imagine your Baba as a child: fighting with her sister, being scolded by her mother or father when she was naughty, or crying her heart out because her best friend did not want to play with her anymore.*

*I have no pictures from my childhood to put in front of you, to make it easier to place me in the stories I want to tell. You will have to use your imagination, and I will try to help you.*

*—H.R.*

memoir

Bits and Pieces

Henia Reinhartz

*Many thanks to my grandson Mordechai Walfish
for his careful reading of the manuscript.*

# CONTENTS

*My family and I were in hiding. The entrance to our*
*hiding place was a wooden wardrobe positioned against a*
*plywood partition.... From dawn until dusk we sat in this*
*little room. We didn't talk.... We were mute, not a sound*
*could be heard, a dead room. We were sure they would*
*discover us.... Suddenly I heard someone panting on the*
*stairs.... We didn't breathe. Who was coming now?*

With her fiery red hair, the teenaged Henele Rosenfarb hides in a
small room in the Lodz Ghetto, in Poland. She is with her parents
and her older sister, and some neighbors who have joined them in
their secret room. Twenty people in all, they try to muffle all
sounds of life, hoping to outwit the Nazi soldiers who have come to
take them to an undisclosed place where they will be killed.

More than half a century later, across a vast ocean, Henele —
now Henia Reinhartz — sits in her home in Toronto. She begins to
write down the stories that comprise the "bits and pieces" of her life,
so that her Canadian-born grandchildren can have a sense of her
childhood and young adulthood, in a different place and a different
time, so unlike their own.

Reinhartz's stories of prewar Poland plunge us into a world of
material poverty, but rich in family warmth, community spirit, passion
for culture, and devotion to social justice. It moves us through the
hardships of World War II and the Nazi genocide, as seen though the
eyes of a young girl. It brings us, eventually, to Montreal of the late

1940s, as experienced by a new immigrant, and finally to Toronto.

Born in 1926 in Lodz, Poland, an industrial city approximately seventy-five miles southwest of Warsaw, Henele was raised in a closely knit extended family that was, in many ways, typical of Polish Jewish families in the early part of the twentieth century. By that time, Jews had lived in Poland for almost a thousand years, and the country had become home to one of the largest Jewish populations in the world.

Jewish life in Poland was full of contradictions. On the one hand, Jewish religious and cultural life had thrived there for hundreds of years. Arriving first as transient peddlers and merchants, Jews eventually settled in Poland to escape the harsh prejudices of the nearby German Empire and other regions. Compared to the Jewish experience elsewhere in Europe and Russia, Polish Jews lived in relative peace with their neighbors. Indeed, the sixteenth century Krakow scholar Rabbi Moses Isserles famously punned on the Hebrew name for Poland — Polin — suggesting that God had led European Jews to the area and told them, "Poh lin," Hebrew for "Rest here." Over centuries, significant centres of Jewish learning and important religious and political movements had developed and flourished. Jews in Poland also evolved their own distinct musical traditions, along with literature, theatre, and cinema in Yiddish, the everyday language of eastern European Jews. On the other hand, Polish Jews often experienced harsh persecution, and sometimes violent attacks — pogroms — at the hands of their non-Jewish Polish neighbors. If Jews were tolerated because, as merchants, middle-men, and financiers, they were perceived as bringing some economic benefit to the country, long-standing prejudices against them nevertheless endured, sometimes erupting in violence. As Polish nationalism developed after World War I, the country became increasingly less tolerant of ethnic minorities in its midst, notwithstanding guarantees in the Polish constitution to protect the rights of minorities. During the period between the two world wars, the economic condition of Polish Jews deteriorated drastically. Barred from most government positions — and the government was a major employer at that time — Jews also found that their usual employments were increasingly taken over by non-Jewish Poles.

By the time Reinhartz was growing up, Polish Jewry was largely urbanized. While some Jews resided in small towns, known as shtetls, by the end of the nineteenth century, most had flocked to the burgeoning cities, partly as a result of government policies regulating their livelihood and residence. Many Polish Jews were deeply pious in their religious practice. But Jews were greatly affected by the process of modernization that was sweeping eastward across Europe. Many of them sought ways to accommodate their traditional ways with secular learning; others began to move away from traditional religious practice, and sought secular ways to define themselves as Jews. Some of these — such as Reinhartz's immediate family — embraced the Yiddish language and Jewish political movements such as the Bund to find more secular ways to identify as Jews.

Shorthand for the *Algemeyner Yidisher Arbeter Bund in Lite, Poyln un Rusland*, or the General Jewish Workers' Union in Lithuania, Poland and Russia, the Bund was a Jewish socialist movement, committed to social justice, the needs of the working person generally, and the special needs of the Jewish worker, in particular (such as the right to refrain from work on the Jewish sacred days). The Bund sought to define a secular Jewish people-hood that focused on the experience and culture of Jews in Eastern Europe. Reinhartz's parents were passionately committed to the ideals of Bund, which provided them with a sense of ethical mission as well as with a social network. Other members of Reinhartz's extended family, such as her Tziotzia (aunt) Adele, Feter (uncle) Yankl and cousin Chava, remained pious in their religious practice, which defined their sense of Jewish identity. Still others embraced Zionism, a political movement that saw a solution to the iv

ongoing persecution of European Jews in resettlement of the historic Jewish homeland — the area that today is the modern country Israel, but in Henia's youth was under British rule. Zionists believed that the fate of Jews would rise and fall according to the whims and political climates in countries where Jews were a minority presence, so long as Jews did not have a country of their own as other nations did. In contrast to the Bund, Zionists placed Hebrew — the language of the Bible and of Hebrew prayer and sacred texts — at the centre of Jewish identity, rather than Yiddish. Still other Polish Jews aspired to advanced degrees and professional careers, sometimes abandoning Yiddish and Hebrew altogether, and integrating into Polish society.

The diversity of religious practice and political views that characterized Reinhartz's extended family and friends was typical of the Jews of Poland at that time. Notwithstanding sharp differences in deeply held beliefs and ideologies, Reinhartz's family — like other Jewish families — remained closely connected, celebrating life events together and looking out for one another. Reinhartz remembers vividly the intense preparation preceding her cousin Chava's wedding, when her mother and aunts spent days cooking for the wedding feast.

Like other children her age, Reinhartz's days were occupied by school and friends, and shaped by her family's association with the Bund. She attended a Bundist school, where the primary language of instruction was Yiddish, and practiced gymnastics at a Bundist gym.

For Henia, this life came to an abrupt end with the German invasion on September 1, 1939. On the eve of the German invasion of Poland, the Jewish population of the country numbered approximately 3.3 million, roughly one tenth of the total population of Poland. By the end of the war, only ten per cent of those Jews remained alive. The Jewish community of Lodz was second in size only to Warsaw, comprising roughly one third of the population of the city. One week after invading Poland, Germany took control of Lodz, renaming it Litzmannstadt. As in all territories controlled by Germany,

Jews suffered immediate consequences. They were compelled to sew yellow six-pointed stars on their clothing, which visibly identified them as Jews. Jewish property was confiscated, Jewish assets frozen, and many Jews forbidden to continue in their jobs or professions. While the inhabitants of Poland generally suffered economically under German occupation, these restrictions hit Polish Jews hardest. It became almost impossible for people to earn sufficient income to feed their families, placing particular strain on families such as that of Reinhartz, economically challenged to begin with.

In February of 1940, half a year after the invasion of Poland, the Germans established a ghetto in the northeast part of Lodz, a restricted area reserved for Jews, who were forbidden to live anywhere else in the city. Throughout Poland, this forced movement of Jewish residents from their homes concentrated the Jewish population in small and bounded areas, intended to house them temporarily before they could be deported to labour camps and deathcamps. Reinhartz's family, along with the other Jews of Lodz, were forced to abandon their homes and most of their possessions, and to move into a rundown section of the city without adequate housing and sewage. Approximately 160,000 people were concentrated in an area far too small to accommodate them. The Nazis hoped that the abysmal conditions, inadequate food supplies, and poor sanitation would demoralize the Jews and quickly reduce their numbers. The resilience of the Jews, physically, psychologically, and spiritually, surprised the Germans.

Of all the ghettoes established by the Nazis, the Lodz ghetto was the most impervious to contact with the outside world. Rather than working outside the ghetto as slave labour, the ghetto inhabitants toiled in factories established within the ghetto walls. Although the Lodz Ghetto published its own newspaper — *The Chronicle* — no outside newspapers were permitted. Radios were confiscated; to possess one was punishable by death. Diaries, too, were forbidden, but many ghetto dwellers, in Lodz and elsewhere, chose to document their experiences by keeping diaries and journals. From accounts of former ghetto dwellers such as Reinhartz, as well as from preserved issues of *The Chronicle* and surviving diaries by Lodz Ghetto residents — most of whom where murdered in the Nazi genocide — we know that ghetto dwellers fought strongly to overcome the attempt to dehumanize and demoralize them. Illegal schools sprung up, as did theatres, cabarets, literary cafes, synagogues, and other aspects of religious and cultural life. While Jewish books had been confiscated and destroyed, Henia's family maintained a clandestine Yiddish library at great personal risk. The Bund continued to be active in the ghetto, providing social structure, schooling, and other types of support. Such forms of spiritual resistance helped sustain the ghetto Jews, even as the Nazi assault on their lives continued relentlessly.

The German Ghetto Administration appointed Chaim Rumkowski, a Lodz Jew, as the "Elder" or head of the ghetto, charged with administering life on a day-to-day basis. The *Judenrat*, or Jewish Council, and the Jewish police reported to him, and he was accountable to the German authorities. Rumkowski operated under strict direction from the German administration, with no real freedom to make decisions that might change the destiny of the Jews in the ghetto. Rumkowski's strategy was to make the Lodz Ghetto indispensable to the economic well-being of Germany. He reasoned that if the factories within the ghetto ran efficiently and productively, the Jews who worked in them would be kept alive indefinitely. "The plan is work, work, and more work!" he announced in a speech. "I will be able to demonstrate, on the basis of irrefutable statistics, that the Jews in the ghetto constitute a productive element."[1] To this end, Rumkowski complied with German demands that those unfit to work — the elderly, the sick, the weaker residents — be rounded up and sent from the ghetto to what many people correctly suspected would be their death.

---

1. Quoted in *The Chronicle of the Łódź Ghetto 1941 - 1944*, p. 115.

But the Germans deliberately deceived the ghetto inhabitants — a deception made easier by the forced isolation of the Lodz Ghetto, which kept them from certain knowledge of mass murder and death-camps. Indeed, even as groups of Jews were taken to from the ghetto to the deathcamp at Chelmno, sixty kilometres away, they were forced to write postcards addressed to relatives and friends remaining in the ghetto, describing their new "home" in glowing terms. These postcards, mailed weeks and months after their writers had been murdered, kept the ghetto dwellers confused about what awaited those deported from the ghetto. Rumkowski's position in history is controversial because of his cooperation with the German authorities, especially in rounding up ghetto dwellers for deportation. In retrospect, it is clear that his strategy to preserve the ghetto could not succeed. Like all Jews under German administration, the Jews of the Lodz Ghetto lived under an inexorable death sentence. At the same time, the Lodz Ghetto lasted longer than any other, destroyed in August, 1944.

Among the last residents of the Lodz Ghetto, Reinhartz was deported to Auschwitz that month, together with her parents and her older sister Chava. From there, the three Rosenfarb women, separated from Henia's father, were taken to a labour camp at Sasel, near Hamburg, Germany. In March, 1945, they were taken forcibly to the concentration camp at Bergen Belsen, where they were liberated by British forces.

Amidst unspeakable suffering and enormous losses, Reinhartz was fortunate to remain with her mother and sister throughout the war years. Many memoirs by women survivors of the Holocaust attest to the importance of the presence of sisters and — especially — mothers. Reinhartz writes repeatedly of her mother's care, even under duress and hardship, and of her enduring closeness with her sister. Their inner strength and mutual support helped them to endure both physically and spiritually. Their lives remained interwoven as they laid roots in Montreal and Toronto. Even as they build their lives anew in a new world, they hold on to much that was important to them in the years before the war. Reinhartz establishes friendships with other Bundists, maintaining the focus on social justice, and nurturing a love of Yiddish language and culture. Her sister Chava Rosenfarb writes Yiddish poetry, drama, and fiction, including her celebrated trilogy of life in the Lodz Ghetto, *The Tree of Life*.

Twice in the memoir, Reinhartz mentions photographs from Poland that adorn her Toronto home. One is of her immediate family — her parents and their two daughters; the other is of her Tziotzia Adele, Feter Yankl, and their five children. For survivors of the Nazi genocide, such photographs are rare treasures. Most Jews of Poland lost all of their possessions. The relatively few Polish Jews who survived the Holocaust were without the heirlooms, souvenirs, and mementos that could connect them to their past. The Rosenfarb family also lost all photographs. Fortunately, relatives who had escaped to Argentina had copies. Those few family photographs are precious in a way hard to imagine in our day of digital and disposable cameras and snapshots.

Yet Reinhartz has managed to paint pictures in language, giving a strong sense of the past, and its place in the present. In recounting the past, Reinhartz's memoir is remarkably free of bitterness and anger. Throughout, Reinhartz focuses on humaneness. Not only does she herself refuse to be dehumanized, but she recollects kindnesses from unexpected quarters, such as Herr Herbert, a German supervisor at a labour camp. As Reinhartz endured life in the ghetto and labour camps, she made two promises to herself: that she would one day become a teacher of Yiddish, and that she would one day live in Paris. Without her explicitly saying so, we come to realize that these two promises carry great symbolic value: an investment in the future, in freedom; an ability to experience life's pleasures once again. Perhaps because it was written with her grandchildren in mind, Henia Reinhartz's memoir reprieves and preserves these moments, and insists that one's ethical values and love for others can outlive the forces that try to snuff them out. In that sense, we might see this memoir in the Jewish tradition of ethical wills, a precious legacy for generations to come.

Sara R. Horowitz
*Toronto, Ontario*
*August 2007*

## Sources

Adelson, Alan and Robert Lapides. *Łódź Ghetto: Inside a Community under Siege*. New York: Viking Penguin, 1989.

Dawidowicz, Lucy. *The War Against the Jews, 1933-1945*. New York: Bantam Books, 1986.

Dobroszycki, Lucjan, ed. *The Chronicle of the Łódź Ghetto 1941-1944*. New Haven: Yale University Press, 1984.

Horowitz, Sara R. "Voices from the Killing Ground," *Voicing the Void: Muteness and Memory in Holocaust Fiction*. New York: State University of New York Press, 1997.

Horowitz, Sara R. "Engendering Trauma Memory," in *Women in the Holocaust*, ed. Dalia Ofer and Lenore Weitzman, New Haven: Yale University Press, 1998.

Mendelsohn, Ezra. "Jewish Politics in Interwar Poland: An Overview," in *The Jews of Poland Between Two World Wars*, ed. Yisrael Gutman. Hanover, New Hampshire: University Press of New England, 1989.

Mendelsohn, Ezra and Isaiah Trunk. "Poland," in *Encyclopaedia Judaica*, 2nd Edition, v. 16, ed. Fred Skolnik. New York: MacMillan, 2006.

Rosenfarb, Chava. *The Tree of Life: A novel about life in the Lodz Ghetto [Der boym fun lebn]*. Melbourne: Scribe, 1985. Republished in three separate volumes by University of Wisconsin Press as: *The Tree of Life [vol. 1]*, 2004; *The Tree of Life: A Trilogy of Life in the Lodz Ghetto: Book Two: From the Depths I Call You, 1940-1942*, 2005; and *The Tree of Life: A Trilogy of Life in the Lodz Ghetto: Book Three: The Cattle Cars Are Waiting, 1942-1944*, 2006.

x

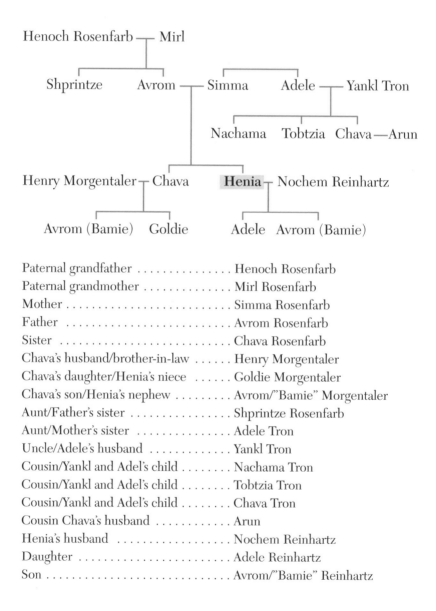

Paternal grandfather . . . . . . . . . . . . . . Henoch Rosenfarb
Paternal grandmother . . . . . . . . . . . . . Mirl Rosenfarb
Mother . . . . . . . . . . . . . . . . . . . . . . . Simma Rosenfarb
Father . . . . . . . . . . . . . . . . . . . . . . . Avrom Rosenfarb
Sister . . . . . . . . . . . . . . . . . . . . . . . . Chava Rosenfarb
Chava's husband/brother-in-law . . . . . . Henry Morgentaler
Chava's daughter/Henia's niece . . . . . . Goldie Morgentaler
Chava's son/Henia's nephew . . . . . . . . Avrom/"Bamie" Morgentaler
Aunt/Father's sister . . . . . . . . . . . . . . Shprintze Rosenfarb
Aunt/Mother's sister . . . . . . . . . . . . . . Adele Tron
Uncle/Adele's husband . . . . . . . . . . . . Yankl Tron
Cousin/Yankl and Adel's child . . . . . . . Nachama Tron
Cousin/Yankl and Adel's child . . . . . . . Tobtzia Tron
Cousin/Yankl and Adel's child . . . . . . . Chava Tron
Cousin Chava's husband . . . . . . . . . . . Arun
Henia's husband . . . . . . . . . . . . . . . . Nochem Reinhartz
Daughter . . . . . . . . . . . . . . . . . . . . . Adele Reinhartz
Son . . . . . . . . . . . . . . . . . . . . . . . . . Avrom/"Bamie" Reinhartz

memoir

Bits and Pieces

**I** **INHERITED MY RED HAIR FROM MY MOTHER**. I remember being upset and angry at her, as red hair was not popular in the Poland of my childhood. Nor did I like my name, Henia. Sometimes children like the sound of someone else's name better. I fell in love with the sound of the name Regina. But of course I was stuck with the name I had and that was that. I was named after my paternal grandfather Henoch. I guess my parents hoped for a boy; instead, this red-haired creature came along as a girl. So my parents changed the name from Henoch to Henia, or, affectionately, "Henele." I do not think my parents were actually disappointed that I was not a boy. They loved me just the way I was. In time, I also came to love my name.

We all have memories that go back to our early lives. My earliest memories are of my mother and father. My mother's name was Simma Rosenfarb. She was not a tall woman and she had red hair. I remember a box stored away with a braid of her hair, and the colour was the same as mine when I was young — a fiery red. She had green-hazel eyes and high cheek bones. Because her colouring did not conform to what was assumed to be a Jewish "look", she didn't suffer the harassment so many other Jews did. Her face expressed wisdom and inner beauty. I loved to look at her. In her eyes, there was always love for me and for everything that was a part of me. She is always present in the memories of my childhood. I think of her as a very wise woman. People liked to be friends with her and sought her counsel. She was the disciplinarian in our family, since she was with us most of the time, while my father was at work.

My mother was a highly skilled mender of textiles. But I saw her working only once. I must have been six or seven. I came home from school to find my father sitting on the couch, his head in his hands, not lifting his eyes to greet me. Our big table was moved to the window and my mother was bent over a big roll of material, mending imperfections with a special needle. I remember being told that my father had lost his job and I recall the sadness on his face and the absolute stillness in the room. It frightened me. This is the only time I remember my mother working. My father probably soon found work, and my mother became busy once again with her two daughters and the household. She was quite strict with us but very loving. Looking back now, I think that she had a pretty good idea how she wanted to raise her children, what values she wanted to instil in us, and what kind of people she wanted us to become. I also remember her as a person with great inner strength and great pride. This became obvious to me during the years of tremendous hardships and pain — during the war years.

As a child I always felt that nothing could happen to me as long as my mother was near. In later years, when I myself was a married woman, she was not only my mother but also a treasured friend. When she died in 1959, I felt orphaned, not only because I had lost my mother, but also because I had lost someone whose love for me was unconditional. After the war, I was always aware of the good fortune and amazing luck to have had her. It was also then that I really understood how much her presence near me during the war helped me to survive. After the war, when I lived in Paris, my mother came from Brussels to live with me. This was a golden opportunity for me to get to know her not only as my mother, but also as a woman. I had so many questions to ask about her own childhood, about her and my father, about some of their friends who peopled my childhood. She liked to share her memories with me and was patient in answering my millions of questions. It was then that we also became great friends.

She was loved by everyone who knew her. Because not too many Jewish mothers survived the Holocaust, she reached out to all our friends and took them under her loving, motherly wings. Pretty soon, everybody was calling her *Mameshi* as a term of endearment, and this is how our friends who knew her refer to her to this day.

When I remember my father, Avrom Rosenfarb, I miss the close relationship we had. I have only childhood and wartime memories of him. He did not come back after the war, and I could not ask the millions of questions I had asked of my mother, so I had no opportunity to forge a friendship with him beyond a father-daughter relationship. But the memories I have of him are filled with love and warmth.

When my children were small and we lived on Glenholme Avenue in Toronto, there stood on our television in the living room a framed photograph of my parents, my sister Chava, when she was about four, and me when I was a few months old (p. 64). This is the only picture I have of my father. When my daughter Adele was a very young girl, she once asked me about the people in this picture. I explained that the woman is her baba Simma, her maternal grandmother, when she was a young mother, her aunt Chava when she was a little girl, and me, her mama, when I was a baby. "But who is this man?" my daughter asked. I explained that this was my father, her zeyde, or grandfather. She could place everyone else. She knew that her baba and aunt Chava lived in Montreal, and that I lived with her here in Toronto. So where was this man who was my tate and her zeyde? I think Adele was two years old at the time. I could not yet tell her that her zeyde perished during the Holocaust. So I simply told her that he lived far away and could not come to us. My wise daughter then asked me, "Does he not want to know what I look like?" "Yes," I replied. "He would want it very much. He just cannot come right now."

My sister Chava and I both named our first-born sons Avrom, "Bamie" for short, after our father. My son Bamie reminds me of my father, though taller. There is a facial, as well as a personality, resemblance. My sister Chava always tells me that she also sees this resemblance in her son. I remember best my father's hands — beautiful, long, white hands. I also remember how elegantly he dressed. It is from him that I believe I inherited my weakness for nice clothes.

He expressed his love for us — his three women, as he liked to call us — in many ways. He liked to kiss and hug us, to carry his daughters piggyback to bed after a bath, to serve all of us breakfast in bed on Saturday mornings, to surprise us with little gifts. He yearned for us to be educated, to reach high, and to become what he could not become: well-educated and independent. Most of all, I remember his kindness, his warmth, and his love for people. I think he was a poet at heart — he just never had the opportunity to express in words the music of his heart. Chava inherited his poetic talent, and became a great Yiddish writer.[1] My own love of and facility with words comes from the same source.

My father was a waiter. I never had the opportunity to ask him why he chose this profession. I think it was because he liked

---

1  Chava Rosenfarb is a Yiddish fiction and essay writer. Her best known work is her trilogy of the Lodz Ghetto, *The Tree of Life: A novel about life in the Lodz Ghetto [Der boym fun lebn]*. Melbourne: Scribe, 1985. Republished in three separate volumes by University of Wisconsin Press as: *The Tree of Life [vol. 1]*, 2004; *The Tree of Life: A Trilogy of Life in the Lodz Ghetto: Book Two: From the Depths I Call You, 1940-1942*, 2005; and *The Tree of Life: A Trilogy of Life in the Lodz Ghetto: Book Three: The Cattle Cars Are Waiting, 1942-1944*, 2006.

people. He liked to be in the midst of conversations and the exchange of ideas, and being a waiter gave him this opportunity. I remember the last place he worked. It was a very elegant restau-rant on Pi-otrkowska Street, the main street of my home town, Lodz.[2] Yiddish writers were steady patrons at the restaurant, and it pleased my father to serve them while listening to their conversations about books and writing. It elated him to be in their company. My father loved to read. I recall sometimes waking up in the middle of the night and seeing him reading in bed by candlelight. We had no table lamps, and he did not want to have the main light on, so as not to wake us. Another memory I have is waking up in the middle of the night and seeing my mother anxiously looking out the window. My father worked until very late at night. People sometimes liked to sit in the restaurant for many hours after they finished their meal, to talk and have a good time. Often he would go to a union meeting after work and come home later than usual. My mother worried. It was rare to have phones in private homes in Poland in those days, so he could not let her know that he would be late.

Sometimes, my friends and I would drop by the restaurant after school. If my father was not busy, he would seat us at a table, let us choose something to eat, and serve us with elegance and grace. At that moment, we were his most precious customers. He always intro-duced me to people whom he knew at the restaurant. "This is my younger daughter, Henele, and these are her friends." I felt very im-portant and loved it, and my friends were terribly impressed. After all, eating in such an elegant restaurant and being served like royalty by a friend's father was not an everyday event for them.

My parents came from the same little town in Poland, Kon-skie, but they both left for the big city when they were quite young. They met and married in Lodz. Lodz was and still is, the second-

---

2  Lodz is spelled Łódź in Polish. For more, see Glossary.

largest city in Poland. It was an industrial city that had the reputation of being a grey, busy place. But it was my hometown and to me it was beautiful. My parents both came from very poor families, and they wanted to break away from the poverty that afflicted many Jewish families in small towns. They thought that in the big city they would be better off. Many young people at that time were drawn to big cities in the hope of improving their lot.

In Lodz, they both joined a political party, the Bund,[3] which had become very popular among Jewish working people. To this day, my husband and I belong to a group comprised of former Bundist members in Toronto. At that time, the Bund was trying to improve the life of Jewish working people. The Bund believed that Jews had rights equal to those of other Polish citizens. In Poland and in other countries, this was not always the case. The Bund maintained that all people had a right to be happy, that wars were bad, that all people — no matter what their colour, race or religion — could live in harmony, and respect each other's differences instead of fighting each other, and that the world could be a beautiful place. This is what my parents learned in the Bund, and the Bund became their second home. There they found many friends who shared those ideas. Thanks to the Bund, my parents' lives became filled with a contentment not known to them in their lives in their small home town. After they married, they structured their home life upon the Bundist values that they so strongly believed in: love, respect for others, the right for Jewish people to develop the Yiddish language and culture, and an opportunity for all citizens to go to school. You see, my parents never went to school. What they knew, they had learned on their own.

This was the home into which Chava and I were born. Chava is almost four years older than I. As a child, I always wanted to go

---

3  The Bund was founded in 1897 in Vilna to fight for the rights of the Jewish worker by combining nationalism and socialism. For more, see Glossary.

wherever she was going. But who wants to drag a little sister along on walks or to a friend's house? Chava did not want to take me along. What did I do? I cried, of course. Did it help me? Of course not. When I was a little older and could go out with my own friends, I stopped pestering her about taking me along.

I remember well our last apartment, the one we lived in until the war broke out. In Poland, most people lived in apart-ment houses. They were built around a square with a courtyard in the middle. The house we lived in was on a very nice street, not far from a park. We lived on the third floor. Our apartment consisted of one huge room and a tiny working kitchen separated from the main room by a thin wooden wall. We had no sink or running water. We had to fetch water from a faucet in the hall. We had no toilet and had to go down to a public toilet in the courtyard. I did not like this, but I still loved our home. I must have been seven or eight years old when we moved there, because I remember going to school by myself already. Whenever I think of my childhood, this home invades my memory and envelops me with light and sunshine, and fragrances from our many plants, and from my mother's cooking and baking. I can see myself doing homework on the big oval table, the table cloth folded, voices from the street coming into the house. There were eight families living on each floor, and each family had children, so I was not lacking in little friends. I sometimes liked to play with my friends in the street. We would skip rope or play other games. While most of the families living in our building were Jewish, there was also one Polish family who lived on our floor. We never talked to them or to their children. I think we were afraid of them. We knew that Poles did not like Jews, and so we stayed away from them.

The school I attended was called the Medem Shul,[4] named after a famous Bundist leader, Vladimir Medem. It was a private school,

---

4 "Shul" is the Yiddish word for school.

8

sponsored by the party to which my parents belonged, the Bund. Except for the Polish language and Polish history, everything was taught in Yiddish. I loved the school and my teachers. They were my models when I, myself, became a teacher. My earliest memory of my school years is from grade one. Our teacher's name was Lererin Hardak. This is how we addressed our teachers: "lerer," for a male teacher, or "lererin," for a female teacher, and then the teacher's name. Lererin Hardak was an elderly woman whom the students loved. We had just begun learning to write with ink. In each desk, there was a round hole for an inkwell into which we would dip our pens. The boy who sat in front of me was named "Indik," which in Yiddish means "turkey." Everybody laughed at him for having such a name. Poor guy. I do not remember what had happened on that particular day — whether the kids were making fun of him and he had had enough of it, or if perhaps I had teased him. All I remember is seeing his hand with the inkwell in it, and seconds later, crying and screaming because he had emptied the inkwell on my head. Picture me: ink dripping from my head, ink all over my clothes, the entire class looking at me, with the boys laughing their heads off, the girls trying to console me. Lererin Hardak came to my rescue. She set me on her desk and tried very hard to clean me up, speaking softly to me the entire time. Finally, she asked a few girls to accompany me home, as there was simply too much ink on me and she could not clean me up. I went home surrounded by four girls, one in front, one in back and one at each side. I must have felt very important: my hair was not red anymore, I went home with escorts, and I was the heroine of the day in my class. Still, I cried and cried. I do not know what happened to this Indik boy or how he was punished. I do not remember going back to school that day, although I am sure I did go back, together with my escorts.

Other school memories involve plays, dancing and singing in the choir. Even though to this day I cannot carry a tune, I am not too bad when I sing with others. I am sure that in my seven years at the

Medem Shul, there were also tears, disappointments, and sadness. However, somehow I do not remember them. Our school was very poor. Although it was a private school supported by the parents, most of them were also poor. Sometimes the school was evicted from its premises for not paying rent, and I remember once people came to take the school piano away. I think ultimately, the piano was saved. Seeing the school's potential loss, someone probably helped out with the money.

Some of the children were extremely poor. Those children did not pay tuition. Every day, a different mother came to the school with ingredients to prepare soup for the needy students. My mother also came to the school twice a week, and busied herself in the kitchen. I loved those days. The kitchen was always open to all the children, so whoever wanted to have a bowl of soup could come in and get one. In this way, the needy children were not singled out. The children loved my mother's soup because it was always made with fat soup bones. I was very proud of her, and was her most faithful customer.

I loved to dance, recite poems, and act. I remember once, on Mother's Day, the school organized an evening of song and poetry dedicated to our mothers. I had a poem to recite. The classroom in which the event took place was decorated with flowers. My mother sat in the first row. As I was reciting my poem, I saw the person behind my mother whispering something into her ear. I also saw my mother's radiant face and heard her whisper back: "This is my younger daughter." I felt pleased knowing that I made my mother proud that evening. This picture is still very vivid in my mind. My teachers felt that I should study drama and spoke with my parents about it. They agreed. I was to enrol in high school after graduation and take drama classes.

My life was very busy. I belonged to the Bundist-run children's organization, the *Sotsyalistisher Kinder Farbund*, or the So-

10

cialist Children's Union, also known as *SKIF*. Like most children who attended the Medem Shul in Lodz, I also belonged to the Bundist sports club, *Morgenshtern*, or Morning Star. I went there twice a week for gymnastics and participated in the club's yearly presentation at the largest theatre in Lodz. I loved it.

High schools in Poland were private and expensive, and therefore not everybody could attend them. When Chava graduated from the Medem Shul, she was coached by a teacher to prepare for an exam that would allow her to enter the second year of high school, thereby saving a year's tuition. When I graduated from the Medem Shul, Chava herself prepared me for such an exam, so that I too, could skip the first year. I gave Chava a hard time because she was my sister. I did not want to listen to her. I passed the exams in all subjects, except German. I had believed that knowing Yiddish, I would certainly pass the German exam, and therefore refused to prepare for it.[5] But of course, Yiddish is not German. Still I was accepted to the second year of high school, but was told that at the beginning of the school year I would have to write the German exam. The beginning of that school year was September 1939; it was also the beginning of the war, when Germany invaded Poland. Schools were still open for a while. I started high school but I did not have to write the German exam. However, drama school was out of the question.

Two other childhood memories stand out in my mind. Someone in my mother's family owned a jewellery store. One day my mother presented me with a little silver ring with a stone in it. I do not recall the colour of the stone, but I remember my joy and pleasure at finally having a real ring, and not one that I had made from paper, string. At night, I slept with the ring and during the day, I played with the ring. I refused to take my eyes off of it. However, one

5  Yiddish is derived from Middle High German, with elements of Hebrew, Aramaic, Romance, and Slavic languages, and written in Hebrew characters. There are similarities between Yiddish and contemporary German.

day, I noticed that the stone was missing. This was a very sad day for me. I was inconsolable. I did not want to look at the ring any more. To me, it had lost its beauty. To this day, whenever I get a new ring, my first silver ring comes to my mind, together with the memory of how much I cherished it, and how sad I was when I lost its stone.

Another memory of my childhood is of my bubeshi, a term of endearment that I use to refer to my paternal grandmother who lived in Konskie, a town in Poland. I saw her only a few times in my life, but I remember her, though I cannot recall her face. I remember her presence rather than what she looked like. She was a small woman, very soft-spoken, and gentle. I had no other living grandparents. My first memory of my bubeshi is from when I was six or seven years old. One summer, my mother took Chava and me to Konskie. Bubeshi lived with her youngest unmarried daughter, our aunt Shprintze, in a room in the attic of an old house. I remember the window of that room because there was such a beautiful view of the garden adjacent to the church and the priest's house. To this day, I remember the mornings that I spent there. I would stand near the open window and take in the perfume smell of the flowers and trees. Being a city child, I was enchanted by it all.

My grandmother and Shprintze had a stall in the market. They sold notions like shoelaces, needles, thread, pins, and other things like that. I remember going with them to the market and being set down in front of a box of blueberries. I was given a pin with which to pick and eat them. I also remember how happy and serene I felt, and the love that my aunt Shprintze and Bubeshi had for me. People were rushing around us, talking in loud voices, and bargaining for goods. Occasionally, somebody would stop at our stall to buy something, and then I could see my grandmother pointing at me and saying, "My Avrom's youngest daughter, Henele." In this small town, people knew each other and they shared my bubeshi's delight in having her grandchildren from the big city stay with her.

The other memory I have of my bubeshi is from a few summers later, perhaps two years before the war. Bubeshi broke a hip at the beginning of the summer and was unable to walk without a cane. My father had rented a cottage in a summer resort near Konskie so that bubeshi could spend the summer with us. My father could not come to see us even once as it was too far and too expensive. My task had been to take bubeshi to the outhouse whenever she needed and whenever I was nearby. I remember her being not much taller than I. She always covered her head, in the manner of religious women. She would hold my arm with one hand while holding onto her cane with the other. I did not feel close enough to my bubeshi to say, "Bubeshi, tell me a story," although I wanted very much to listen to her stories and knew she had many. Our father was always telling us that she came from an old family of Jewish scholars and writers.

I had many aunts and uncles. Some lived in Konskie and others in Lodz. I loved my father's sister Shprintze from Konskie, and my mother's older sister Adele, the best. I named my own daughter after Adele. Shprintze was young, at most in her early twenties. She had dark wavy hair, dark eyes, and a lovely voice. I thought she was beautiful. From time to time she would come to Lodz to buy merchandise for their stall and stay with us. I remember her being full of fun, laughter, and songs. I suppose for a while she would forget the heavy responsibilities she carried at home. I remember her wedding shortly before the war. It was in our home, so the groom must have been from Lodz. My mother prepared the food with the help of some friends. I remember the furniture pushed to the walls to make room for the long tables. I do not recollect much of that wedding. However, I remember that the marriage was arranged by a matchmaker. I recall that I did not like the groom, and to me, our Shprintze's face seemed sad. This is the last memory I have of her.

We called my mother's sister Tziotzia, or "aunt" in Polish, Adele. She looked a lot like my mother but wore a wig as she was a very religious woman and kept a traditional home. We adored her and she loved us very much. Her husband's name was Feter, or "uncle" in Yiddish, Yankl. Feter Yankl and Tziotzia Adele had five children: four daughters and one son. The two youngest daughters were the same age as Chava and I. I have only one photograph of them all (p.64). Our two families were very different. Ours was secular. We did not go to synagogue or observe religious holidays, whereas Tziotzia Adele's home was very observant. Yet we loved one another and respected each the other's way of life.

My warmest childhood memories are connected with my Feter Yankl and Tziotzia Adele's family and their home. Every *Shabbes*, or Sabbath, we would go to their house. They lived quite far from us in Baluty, an area of Lodz with a large Jewish population. Later, during the war, this part of the city became the Jewish ghetto, but by then, my Tziotzia Adele was no longer living there. It was our custom that Tobtzia, the cousin closest to my age, would go with me to fetch the *tsholent* that Tziotzia Adele had made for *Shabbes*, from the baker. *Tsholent* is a dish of meat and potatoes served on *Shabbes* and kept overnight in the baker's stove. There were always many people invited for the *Shabbes* meal at the table, including friends of my cousins and family. The table seemed to have the capacity to accommodate everybody. My older cousins belonged to a Zionist organization, while we belonged to the Bund, so there were always discussions at the table because the two movements had very different ideologies.[6] There was a lot of singing and talking at the table. I loved them all so much. They were hard-working people who earned their living by making socks on little machines in their home. Tziotzia Adele spun the yarn and Feter Yankl sold the socks to local stores. All seven of

---

6  Although Zionism and Bundism were both Jewish national movements and served as Jewish political parties in interwar Poland, Zionism advocated a Jewish national homeland in the Land of Israel, while Bundism advocated Jewish cultural autonomy in the Diaspora. For more, see Glossary.

them lived in one room with a kitchen in which they also worked. In an adjacent room lived Feter Yankl's parents. On *Shabbes*, the machines were put away, and the home cleaned and made festive. They all occupy a special corner in my heart, and sometimes when I feel lonely, I retreat to that corner to warm myself in memories of my Tziotzia Adele and her family.

I was eleven yearsold when Tziotzia Adele and Feter Yankl's daughter Chava got married. My mother was to help with the wedding preparations, so we went to stay at Tziotzia Adele's house the week before the wedding. I hardly recognized the surroundings. Tziotzia Adele wore a large coloured apron, with her sleeves rolled up, while supervising the huge pots and pans on the stove. In all the excitement, her wig slid down, and a few of her own hairs were revealed. Feter Yankl prayed and kept out of the way as much as he could. The wedding was to take place in the house, and for a week, it seemed as though Tziotzia Adele and my mother never left the kitchen. The hall door stayed ajar and there was a continuous flow of relatives and neighbours coming in and out, tasting the food, giving advice, and helping to remove the furniture. It was hard not to be under someone's feet in what felt like a beehive.

I could hardly wait until the wedding day. I wanted to wear my new dress and shoes made especially for the occasion, but most of all I was curious to meet my new cousin, Chava's future husband. I wondered: Was he handsome? Was he young? Would he discuss politics like the boyfriends of my other cousins, or would he, like Feter Yankl, devote his free time to the love of God?

My cousin Chava was my aunt and uncle's eldest daughter. With yellowish hair, a light complexion, and watery blue eyes, she was not as good-looking as her brothers and sisters. However, she was tall, slim, and very graceful. Shy and withdrawn, she never joined them in song or chatter. She remained aside, while the others sang songs filled not with belief in the Messiah, but with belief that they themselves could be Messiahs and change the world. She could not cross that bridge, like the others had, from the old to the new. The old was familiar to her, and she knew her place in it. The blessing of the *Shabbes* candles and the chant of her father's prayers formed the rhythm of her life. She felt that she was a link in a long chain, like her mother, and like her grandmother before her. She was afraid to break this chain.

Tziotzia Adele accepted the changes in her children with tolerance, as long as there was no open rebellion and defiance against religion, and as long as traditions and customs were respected. My cousin Chava accepted the gap between her and her siblings with resignation. I loved and looked up to them all. I admired their skill in operating the hand-knitting machines they used to make the men's socks. They spoiled me.

We lived quite a distance from them. It was a tradition in my family to walk to Tziotzia Adele's almost every Saturday to join in their festive meal around the large table where I was "the child." Later, as synagogues were burned down in my hometown, and in other Polish towns, we could no longer reach Aunt Adele's dinner table. It was then that I knew that my childhood had ended.

At this table one Saturday, I eavesdropped on a conver-sation between my mother and Tziotzia Adele:

"Chava is seeing the young man tomorrow. The match-maker, Mr. Rubin, arranged it. According to Mr. Rubin, he comes from a fine family and is a learned and fine man himself," Tziotzia Adele whispered into my mother's ear.

"Does Chava still resent the matchmaking?"

"You know Chava," Aunt Adele sighed. "I do not know what is with this girl. First she said that she will never in her life marry a man picked for her by a matchmaker, then she shouted at me in anger that she would do so, and sacrifice herself for the others".

"Is this how she feels about it? Poor girl," my mother said.

"Stupid she is not. She knows well that her sisters will not marry their boys until she, being the eldest, is led with God's will to the *chuppah*, the wedding canopy. And she is right…but how much longer must the others wait? It is time for them too to get married." And Tziotzia Adele wiped a tear away with her apron.

"I hope he pleases her, Adele. She deserves happiness." My mother's eyes were moist too.

I remembered this conversation during the nights when I slept at Tziotzia Adele's. I shared a bed with my cousin Chava and my mother slept with my aunt because they wanted to talk about work that still needed to be done. Everyone said it was a privilege to sleep with a bride before her wedding, but I was not happy about it. Night after night I was awakened by Chava's sobs. My intuition told me to pretend I was asleep, but I was worried.

"Ma," I asked my mother one morning, "Why does Chava cry every night?" My mother looked at me and said quietly, "Some girls just feel that way before their marriage."

"Did you cry too, before you married Tate?"

"It was a long time ago, little daughter. I do not remember."

Finally the day came. The two rooms on both sides of the kitchen were ready. The throne-like chair at the head of the women's table was guarded by tall plants, like two soldiers waiting for a queen. The throne was for Chava, for on that day, she was queen. She looked beautiful that evening. Very pale after a day's fasting, she seemed taller than usual in her long white dress. The bride was the only one dressed in white, and, among the happy faces of arriving guests, Chava looked like a birch-tree in a strange forest. It was already after the ceremony, but there were still people coming. The noise was a mixture of tears, laughter, and chatter. I was kissed on the cheeks constantly. My mother seemed to know everyone as she shook hands, accepted wedding gifts, and the customary congratulatory tidings, "*Mazl-tov*, with God's will at your daughter's wedding." "*Mazl-tov* and the same to you," my mother replied. Chava smiled at the guests uneasily, her smile mixed with tears. It seemed to me that her tears never stopped flowing, and they marred my happiness.

I did not know yet whether the groom was handsome or whether I liked him as a husband for my cousin. I hardly caught a glimpse of him. I was present in the yard when Chava joined him under the *chuppah*. My importance, however, was completely ignored by the stout matrons who blocked my view of the spec-tacle. But I peeked into the room where the men were sitting. They were eating heartily and singing. They clapped their hands to the rhythm of their singing, their beards and *peyes*, or side curls, moved up and down, as though dancing in harmony. My father served the food, bringing in plates arranged evenly along his left arm. He looked like a dancer performing a ritual dance, with his right hand moving gracefully to the left arm and removing a plate, placing it in front of guests, all the while keeping rhythm with the singing of the guests. Feter Yankl sat at the head of the table in his new black coat, with his long greyish beard neatly combed. He called me over. I felt shy in front of all these large men behaving like children. I went straight to the top of the table into the safety of Feter Yankl's lap.

"You didn't wish me *mazl-tov*, little girl. An uncle deserves a kiss on such an occasion," he said.

"*Mazl-tov*, Feter Yankl." As I kissed him, I laughed because his whiskers tickled me.

"Say *mazl-tov* to your new cousin, Arun, Chava's husband," and he motioned to his right.

"Ah, so that's what he looks like," I thought as I tried to take him in. "*Mazl-tov*, cousin Arun," I said shyly.

"*Mazl-tov*, little cousin, with God's will at your wedding," he said and smiled at me. His eyes seemed to say, "I am not so serious all the time, do you think I am all right for a cousin?" I thought so. He seemed fine to me. I wanted to run to Chava and tell her not to cry any-more, for I met her groom and he seemed really nice and I liked him.

I went back to the room where the women were celebrating and waved happily to Chava. She waved back to me, the wedding band shinning on her finger. Tziotzia Adele moved from guest to guest, urging them to eat more, accepting compliments on the food, and good wishes for the young couple. The women sang and danced as well, and the songs mixed nicely with the Hassidic tunes from the other room. Suddenly, someone pointed to the kitchen and said, "Quiet, everybody quiet. Avrom is going to make a speech."

My father stood on an empty beer barrel with his beautiful white hands outstretched, facing the room in which the men were sitting. He looked young and handsome in his new suit, a gleaming white shirt, and dark bow tie. His *kippa,* or skull cap, gave him an air of solemnity. "Arun, son of Isaac," my father began, "it is to you whom I want to speak. It is you whom I want to welcome into the family of our sister Adele. You are a fortunate man, Arun, for you come into a home where love dwells. Love of God, to be sure, but also love of man. You are coming into a home where the hungry are fed and the thirsty given drink. Whoever comes to this house sick and upset leaves it comforted and happier. This is Adele's special gift. Our sister Adele is not rich. She spends her days at the spinning wheel here in this kitchen, preparing yarn for the socks that her children make. Yet she is richer than many women, for she has managed over the years to become the owner of a rare and unique piece of jewellery. This is a string of five beautiful pearls, Arun. She takes care of them with love and tenderness, and wears them with humility but pride. She has entrusted you, Arun, with one of her pearls. See that you are worthy of it. Love it and take care of it, and you can be sure of becoming the sixth pearl on our sister Adele's string."

A hush fell over the room followed by loud applause. Then someone broke out into the traditional Polish song, "A hundred years, a hundred years may he live a hundred years." How were they to know that the concentration camp Dachau would cut his life to much less than half that many.

I looked at my father, standing among the guests shaking their hands, and suddenly I realized that my father was no ordinary man. He was a poet, a real poet, I thought with pride. My Tziotzia Adele came to him with outstretched hands. He took both of her hands into his, kissed her cheek, and said, "May you know only joy." She looked up at him, eyes filled with tears, and only whispered, "Avrom…Avrom…," too moved to say anything more. Chava came forward to my father and embraced him, "That was a beautiful speech, Uncle." "And you are a beautiful bride," my father replied. "Chava, you will be happy, he is a good man." My father, the gallant man he was, kissed her hand and as he did so, he saw that her wedding ring was missing. "Your ring?" he whispered into her ear. She looked at her hand and her face went white, whiter than the wedding dress. "It must have slipped. I lost it, I did not want to," she murmured in panic as she bent down beside my father to look for it. People soon realized what had happened, and suddenly all I could hear was one word: Ring.

"Lost the ring."
"Find the ring."
"Where is the ring?"
"Don't tell the groom about the ring."
"The ring, the ring, the ring…"

The ring was finally found and returned to Chava. It was late. I was sleepy and tired. Before going to bed I went over to Chava and asked, "Will the others get married soon?" Quickly realizing that I should not have asked this, I added, "I am going to like your husband. Cousin Arun is a nice man." Chava kissed me and smiled, the first real smile on her face that evening. This was the last festive event and the last family gathering in my Tziotzia Adele's home. It was the last happy family event of my childhood.

I am certain that my childhood years had all kinds of days — sunny, happy, and also sad days. Sometimes my parents were angry with me, sometimes I was angry with myself, and sometimes I was angry with them. Sometimes I felt pain, disappointment, and frustration. However, when I think about my childhood years now, I feel warmth around me and the memory of great security attached to it. I remember a loving home, parents who loved each other very much, and loved us, their children. They served as my example when I raised my own children. I tried to pass on to them what I learned at home from my parents. I am grateful to my parents for the example they gave me, and for their love.

I graduated from the Medem Shul in June 1939. Graduation was an exciting event, though it was accompanied by disappointment. I knew I was a candidate for a very prestigious prize the school awarded each year to the best student. Chava had received the prize when she graduated. However, the year I graduated, the prize went to a boy in our class. Naturally, I was upset. At that time, I already knew I had been accepted to the second year of high school. I was very happy about this and it softened my disappointment. Little did I know that my whole life was about to be turned upside down.

The war broke out on 1 September 1939, when Germany invaded Poland. The Germans occupied our city in the first days of the war. Lodz had a large German population that welcomed the occupiers with open arms. I began high school apprehensive and fearful. Everyone understood that the Germans would not allow Jewish schools to remain open. Indeed, after a short while, the order came to close them. My school days seemed to be over.

My first encounter with Nazi cruelty came very soon. I was standing near the window of our apartment, watching my father cross the street to get to a store to change some money. To my horror, I saw two German soldiers approach him, push him, and order him to walk in front of them. I immediately ran out and begged the soldiers to let him go. I pleaded with them, telling them that he was my daddy and that they could not do this to him. They laughed, pushed me away, collected a few more Jewish men, and marched them off toward the city centre. I marched beside them, together with my mother and some other Jewish women. The men were forced to dig trenches in the middle of the city until late that night. When my father was released, we ran home through the empty streets. My sister Chava was waiting for us with a hot meal. From that moment on, my father never left the apartment. We were constantly on the lookout, and when we would see German soldiers rounding up Jewish men and dragging them from their homes, we would run home and lock my father in the apartment. They never took my father again.

On the ground floor of our house was a bakery owned by an elderly German couple. During the first days of the war, they would sell loaves of bread to their neighbours. They did it before opening the store, so that neighbours would not have to queue up a whole night in order to get bread. This helped us a lot. We would buy four loaves of bread and could exchange some for eggs and butter. Food was already scarce, and what was available was quite expensive. Even before the war began, people were discussing food shortages. My father told us that he had taken our winter shoes to the shoemaker to make hiding places in the shoes' heels for money and for my mother's golden watch, her only valuable piece of jewelry. He wanted each of us to have some money in case we were separated. I do not know how much money we had, but I am sure it was not a lot. Nor did we know how long the war would last.

After a while our German neighbours stopped being generous to their Jewish neighbours, and we had to line up like everyone else. The store opened in the morning, but people began to line up the evening before. One evening, we went down to join the line. My father stayed behind, locked in the apartment. I stood behind my mother, with my sister Chava behind me. Early the next morning, the doors opened and the line advanced in a slow but orderly fashion. I was not far from the door when suddenly a German soldier with a little Polish boy, not more than five or six years old, appeared.

The little boy pointed at me, telling the soldier, *"Jude! Jude!"* (Jew!
Jew!). The soldier kicked me out of the line. I ran home and said
nothing to my father. I threw myself on the bed, tears streaming
from my eyes. I could not stop crying. My world was collapsing and
nothing was the same anymore. I was bewildered and could not understand what had just happened. I was humiliated and angry. I could
not control my rage. My mother came up and tried to console me.
"Don't cry, you see, I have two loaves. I took one and hid it under my
shawl and then went to the other salesman and got another one, for
you. Don't cry." The finger of that little Polish boy pointing at me,
telling the German soldier that I was a Jew pierced my twelve-year-old
heart. To this day, I still feel this hurt.

As soon as the Nazis conquered Poland and other European countries, they made the Jews wear yellow armbands or yellow stars with
the word "*Jude.*" In Lodz, we had to wear two yellow stars. One star
was attached to the front of the garment and the other to the back.
We were not permitted to go outside without them. To appear in the
street without the yellow stars meant heavy punishment, even death.

The Germans annexed Lodz, and changed its name to Litzmannstadt, making it officially a part of Germany, and no longer a
part of Poland. The mood in our home was gloomy. We did not know
what to expect. We could no longer move freely around the city. We
were afraid. Some of my friends left the city with their parents, to
Warsaw or to other places. In those first months of the war, I lost
touch with most of my friends, and I missed them.

On a bitterly cold winter day at the beginning of 1940, we
heard rumours that German soldiers were rounding up and evacuat-
ing the Jews from the area where Tziotzia Adele lived. We did not believe the rumours, and my mother and I walked to Tziotzia's house.
It was just unthinkable that she would not be there. However, the rumours were true. There were soldiers all over the street, and we
could not even get close to the house. I never saw Tziotzia Adele or
Feter Yankl or my cousins again. Only Nachama, one of my cousins,
and her family remained. They were later relocated to the ghetto.

---

7   Jews were forced to live in ghettoes under Nazi rule. These areas consisted
    of cramped conditions in a specified and enclosed area of a city. See Glossary
    for more.

The ghetto in Lodz was located in the small, dilapidated district of Baluty, which was heavily populated by Jews, and where my Tziotzia Adele used to live. All the Jews of Lodz, over 230,000 of us, were forced to squeeze into this area. It was the winter of 1940. It was a very cold winter. Through the icy streets, under dark unfriendly skies, a constant stream of Jews moved from all over the city into the ghetto. We were among them. We were given only a few days to leave our home. Of our possessions, we took only what we could carry. We had to leave behind all our furniture. We were allowed to open Tziotzia Adele's empty apartment, and we moved in. How strange it was to be in this home without the people I loved so much. Our neighbours, a family of three, and two distant cousins came to live with us. They had nowhere else to go.

With so many people in such a small area, the ghetto was terribly crowded. Soon it was closed off, surrounded with barbed wire fence. No one was permitted to leave or enter. The various parts of the ghetto, which were separated from each other by a thoroughfare, were connected by bridges that crossed above the thoroughfare. Soldiers guarded the ghetto outside the barbed-wire fence. We were completely isolated from the outside world. That was what the Germans wanted.

The place became even more crowded when the Germans brought in Jews from neighbouring towns, and later from Germany and Czechoslovakia. Slowly, some kind of order was established. The Germans appointed a Jew, Chaim Rumkowski, as head of the ghetto. In turn, he appointed people to aid him in administering services. He also recruited a Jewish police force to keep order. He opened stores called co-operatives, in which the meagre food rations that the Germans allotted for the Jews were distributed. My father worked in such a store. His ties with the Bund helped him obtain this work. He was not allowed to bring anything home from the co-operative, but he was able to nibble on some food while there. To help his family, he ate at work when he could, and thus did not touch his food ration at home, which left a little more food for the rest of us.

We had to leave Tziotzia Adele's apartment soon after we moved into the ghetto. The ghetto administration took over the building for offices. We were given another apartment on Lagiew-nicka Street, number eight, on the other side of the bridge. This apartment had one room divided by a thin plywood wall into a kitchen area and a small bedroom. We were finally by ourselves. No one else lived with us. We remained in this apartment until the liquidation of the ghetto in August 1944.

Before the Germans destroyed the Yiddish library, the *Groyse-bibliotek*, a group of Bundists managed to rescue a number of its books. These were brought to our apartment. It was a policy of Nazi Germany to burn Yiddish and Hebrew books, as well as books by Jewish writers and political opponents. My sister Chava and I, along with the help of a few friends, sorted and catalogued the rescued books. Shelves were put up in the kitchen to house them. Our kitchen thus became the ghetto library.[8] This was an underground library, which means that it was kept secret, so that neither the ghetto administration, nor the Germans were to know about it. The library mostly served those affiliated with the Bund, both young and old. However, when other people heard about it and came to us, they, too, were allowed to take out books. I loved working in the library. People read a lot in the ghetto. My love for books and reading stems from that time. Reading meant escaping into another world, living the lives of the heroes and heroines, sharing their joys and sorrows, the joys and sorrows of a normal life, in a normal world unlike ours, full of fear and hunger.

---

8   Other lending libraries also remained in the Lodz Ghetto, including Sonenberg's lending library, as well as other smaller lending libraries that existed in private apartments. Isaiah Trunk, *Lodz Ghetto: A History*. Bloomington: Indiana University Press, 2006, p 339.

The Bund and other political parties reorganized in the ghetto, and life seemed to settle into a certain rhythm. While hunger and disease were rampant, at least we did not have to look at the faces of the Nazis, and we no longer had to get off the sidewalk when a German was approaching. The Germans avoided coming into the ghetto for fear of catching a disease. Once again, I was surrounded by my friends. We all became citizens of the ghetto. We participated in its everyday life, and shared its sadness and its hope that perhaps one day, we would see the end of the ghetto and the Nazis.

The Bund, with all of its branches, was now divided into five groups for security reasons. Each group had a leader who was responsible for the group and its activities. We met at least once a week. Most of my friends were young Bundists like myself, with whom I spent all my free time. The Bund, like all organized ideological movements in the ghetto, was very active. We organized lectures on various topics in one of the Bundist-run soup kitchens.[9] For a while, there was an orchestra and a theatre about which only the ghetto population knew. These too, were secret, underground institutions. Each time there was a performance, the place was guarded by people on the lookout for German soldiers. We did not want the Germans to know that we were fighting back by keeping our spirits alive and hopeful. We organized a support network for our many friends who were sick, and for the many who had lost their families. We were sometimes called upon to share our meagre rations with a sick friend or with a friend hiding to escape deportation.

Not every day in the ghetto was gloomy. There were days of respite when there were no *Aktionen* (actions), that is, deportations of people from the ghetto to an unknown destination. Or when spring came and we were no longer freezing in our homes or on our way to

9  Public kitchens in the Lodz Ghetto were operated by Jewish political parties that had been active in interwar Poland. Isaiah Trunk, *Lodz Ghetto*, p 335.

work, and when buds appeared on the few trees, and we could hear birds singing. Those were days when we rejoiced. Spring was our great comforter, filling us with hope and with a promise of survival. Away from the centre but still part of the ghetto, was the district of Marysin, which consisted of empty fields covered with grass.[10] This was our favourite gathering place in the spring. My friends and I would go to Marysin on Sundays when the factories were closed, and pretend that we were free, and sing our hearts out.

---

10 Marysin was an area of small farms and houses that was annexed to the Lodz Ghetto in May 1940.

# THE *SPERRE*

**Hunger and disease were our constant companions in the ghetto,** but as long as there were no deportations and no Germans, our spirits did not surrender. We refused to give up hope that we would live to see better days. This hope was difficult to nurture when there were deportations since nobody knew whose turn it would be next to be taken away.

The most nightmarish action in the ghetto took place in September 1942. It became known as the *Sperre*, which in German means "closing". For ten days, we were not allowed to leave our homes. First, on 1 September, the Germans liquidated the one hospital that had remained in the ghetto. Then they went from house to house and ordered everyone out. We were forced to assemble in the courtyards where the selection took place. The Germans took children, elderly people, and those who were not to their liking. They forced them into trucks and took them away. There was hardly a home that remained untouched. What I remember most from those ten days was the screaming, the lament that rose from all the homes, from all corners of the ghetto. I also remember running with my father at night to hide in a part of the ghetto where the selection had already taken place. I can also recall the book I was reading, *Gone with the Wind* in Polish translation. I sat on the floor, somewhere in a corner, with my fingers in my ears to shut out the screaming world around me, trying to escape the fear and the pounding in my heart. It was at that time that I became sick with typhus. However, we were lucky to still be alive. Our close family was gone, the last trace of my Tziotzia Adele. So many of our friends were taken away. The ghetto was decimated. For a while, it seemed that our spirits were broken, and that we had given up. But after a while, we dared to hope again, to dream, and to fight for survival.

At first the Germans allowed schools to open in the ghetto, including one high school. Many children enrolled since the high school was free. We received an extra piece of bread at school, thanks to the head of the ghetto, Chaim Rumkowski. This helped to attract students. The school was like heaven for me and everyone else who attended. I would meet my friends early in the morning and walk to school. Our classrooms were scattered over many little houses. Some were miles from the heart of the ghetto. School was a world without war and without Germans. Cold and hunger were forgotten. We were eager to learn. Our teachers were gentle and understood us. They, too, were hungry and cold. They were completely devoted to their work, and they encouraged us and gave us hope.

But the ghetto schools had a short life. The Germans did not want Jewish children to study, to attend school, or even to have a little fun. Everyone had to work, and children from the age of ten became part of the workforce. The ghetto Jews worked for the Germans. Factories were established where uniforms were produced for the German soldiers, furniture for German families, and wooden toys for German children. There were factories that produced leather goods, and laundries that washed the Nazis' dirty linen. Because we were working for them, the Germans allowed some food into the ghetto.

Children also worked in those factories, but they studied as well. The German order to close the schools was not obeyed. The schools went underground. Their existence became a secret between the teachers and students. The teachers divided their students into groups of five. Older students who were taught by teachers, in turn, taught the younger students. Teaching took place in homes and at the workplace. I was given a group of young children to teach. I taught them mostly at work during breaks, since my group of five children worked at the same factory. It was then that I promised myself that if I survived the war, I would dedicate my professional life to teaching Yiddish to children.

I worked in the painting section of a carpentry shop where we made furniture and wooden toys for the Germans. We had to wear overalls and masks, as the toys were sprayed with paint. The mist was toxic and would fill our nostrils and affect our breathing. Still, I loved working there because of the people with whom I worked. We were a group of fifteen and we always worked together, one week on the day shift, and one week on the night shift. I was the youngest, yet I was chosen to be the repre-sentative of the group. We became like one big family, helping each other and looking out for each other.

I remember the day when one of our workers did not show up for work because she was on the list of people to be deported from the ghetto. We did not know at that time where the deportees were taken or what would happen to them. Nobody wanted to be sent out from the ghetto where we still had a roof over our heads and were on familiar grounds. Our co-worker decided to hide. However, while in hiding, she was unable to receive her food rations. During our break, we would gather in a little room adjacent to the big hall to eat our soup and talk. On that particular day, we came to the room with our soup, and found a pot on the table. We understood what it meant, and each contributed a few spoonfuls of soup to help her out during her difficult days of hiding.

The work we did was considered harmful to our health. Not that the Nazis cared, but rumour had it that Rumkowski, the head of the ghetto, would grant an extra soup for work he considered harmful to one's health. We decided to try our luck. An extra soup a day was worth fighting for. As the representative of our shift, I was to meet with Rumkowski when he visited the factory. I went to the director of the factory, who was also a Bundist, and whose niece was a high school friend of mine. I asked him to arrange a meeting with Rumkowski. One day, I was called to his office. I went to meet him wearing my dirty, paint-smeared overalls, with my mask hanging from my neck. I was very nervous and afraid of Rumkowski, as was everyone. One never knew what crazy ideas he might have and how he would treat you, either with a slap in the face or with a smile. I remember the first question he asked was whether I had a fiancé. Speaking very quickly, I told him that no, I had no fiancé, that I came on behalf of the workers of the toy painting department and that due to the dirty air we were breathing, the work made us sick. I told him that we were good workers, and that we liked the work, and asked if he could recommend us for an extra soup. I then thanked him. We received the second ration of soup and, for a short while, also a glass of milk. We rejoiced, as this was a victory.

FRIENDSHIP

Friendship is the most wonderful gift people can share. This was particularly true for me in the ghetto. With my friends, I shared my dreams and hopes for a time without Nazi Germany and war. We would talk about books, boys, love, and nice clothes. We all belonged to the Bundist youth movement, *SKIF*. A lot of my pre-war friends did not enter the ghetto. Some left with their parents for other Polish towns, while others went to Russia with their parents. Among my closest friends in the ghetto were Rushka, who now lives in Beer-Sheva, Israel, and a beautiful girl named Sorele Kornblum. Sorele, her little brother, and their parents, were among the first taken from the ghetto. Her father was unable to find work in the ghetto, and thus her family lived on an allowance from the administration. Those on assistance were the first to be deported. At the time, we thought they were being relocated. Much later, we learned the truth. They were among the first to be killed by poison gas in trucks built for that purpose, in Chelmno,[11] not far from Lodz. Sorele's deportation was the first time I felt a deep loss while in the ghetto.

My closest friend in the ghetto was Chanale Hauser, a class-mate of mine. We worked at the same factory, however she worked in the office in my department. She lived close to us with her step-mother, father, younger sister, and older brother. The two of us were

---

11 Chelmno was a deathcamp sixty kilometres from Lodz. For more, see Glossary.

inseparable. We organized artistic programs for the Bund, together with the children from *SKIF*. Chanale's home was a gathering place for young people. Her brother Motl was very active in the Bund, and his friends met in their house. Our friend Bono Wiener secretly kept a radio receiver in a canteen. Had the Germans caught him, he would have been sentenced to death. He would bring news from the outside world to our secret meetings. He would listen to BBC radio from England and inform us about the happenings on the outside. We would hang on to these bits and pieces of news, discussing and interpreting them, though not always accurately, but always with an effort to find something hopeful, something to give us courage.

There was a curfew in the ghetto. We were forbidden to be in the street from early evening until dawn. During our first winter in the ghetto, all of the wooden fences between the houses disappeared. The wood was used for heat and as fuel to cook the meagre meals from our rations. Therefore, without fences separating the buildings, we were able to move freely from house to house despite the curfew. It was as though after curfew life in the ghetto moved from the streets to the backyards.

While in the ghetto I became sick with typhus, and was bedridden for six weeks with a high fever. I was constantly thirsty. I kept dreaming about the blue pot in our home before the war that was always filled with cold drinks for the children. The Bund saved my life. I needed a daily injection of medicine that was difficult to obtain in the ghetto. Miraculously, Bundist members managed to get the medicine to me every day. A distant cousin of mine, who was a nurse, came by every day to give me the injection. My friends would come to the door with little notes for me, as they were not allowed in since typhus is very contagious. When I went outside for the first time after my recovery, my mother had to teach me how to walk again. Chanale was the first to greet me. I saw Chanale for the last time a day before we were taken from the ghetto.

# THE LIQUIDATION OF THE GHETTO

We knew the Russian army was advancing and liberation was close. We desperately wanted to stay in the ghetto. We knew that if we could stay, we would soon be liberated. But the Germans had other plans for us. In the middle of August 1944, the Germans ordered all Jews to be removed from the ghetto. Each day, a certain number of people would be deported. The Germans promised a loaf of bread to those who voluntarily presented themselves. Very few people went. Bread was no longer enticing, freedom was.

Recently, I came across an article I wrote after the war for *Unzer Shtime*, or "Our Voice," a Bundist-run Yiddish daily newspaper published in Paris. I wrote the article in August 1946, exactly two years after the liquidation of the Lodz Ghetto. At the time, I was living in Brussels. Re-reading the article now, brings back the sounds and the smells of the ghetto in those last nightmarish days. Here are some excerpts from my article, which I have translated into English:

> *It has been ten days and the ghetto is in a feverish state. During the day, the ghetto seems dead, except for the Germans who run from street to street to collect their victims. Nobody is going voluntarily. Each nook, each basement, each attic, hides the secret of hidden lives. Children remain silent as Nazi boots bang on doors. Only their eyes convey their dread. Their little fingers*

*digging into their mothers' flesh speak their fear, pain,
their hatred of the boots, and their love for the only person
who they think can save them, their mother. In order to get
people to come willingly, Biebow, the German in charge of
the ghetto, had communicated that we would only be going
to another work camp because the Germans do not want to
deliver us to the Russians. Nobody believed him. We knew
better for we already knew about the concentration camps
and the chimneys. We wanted to stay.*

*At night, the ghetto could breathe a little easier. The Germans
did not work at night. People would come out of their
hiding places to get some fresh air, stock up on water, see
who was taken away and who was left, and perhaps to find
some of the food left behind in the emptied homes. I met
Chanale every evening. We knew these were our last days
together, and we did not know what lay ahead. We were
afraid. The dreams and hopes that we had nurtured for
so long and had refused to give up had abandoned us,
and were replaced by despair.*

*My family and I were in hiding. The entrance to our hiding
place was a wooden wardrobe positioned against a plywood
partition separating the bedroom from the kitchen. We hid
in the bedroom. There were twenty of us. Some of our
neighbours and their little children also hid here. The door
of our third-floor apartment had been locked from the
outside by a sick neighbour whose wife and daughter we
hid with us. He did not want to hide any more. The
Germans came by here every day. From dawn until dusk
we sat in this little room but did not talk. We tried not to
listen to what went on underneath our window in the
courtyard. The Germans had broken through the door*

of our apartment unit several times already. They had
ransacked the room but did not notice the thin wall.
Therefore, they were unaware that behind the wardrobe,
twenty pairs of eyes were glued to the hidden entrance,
and twenty pairs of ears picked up their every movement.
We were mute, not a sound could be heard, a dead room.
But then we heard them open the door to the wardrobe and
rummage through. We were sure they would discover us.
We began to get up, but my father's eyes commanded us to
remain seated. Eventually they left, and a small commotion
followed. We whispered to each other. We did not dare to
speak loudly, afraid of our own voices. Our building was
already empty. We were the only ones left. We were afraid,
but also happy that another day had passed and we were
still in our home. A spark of hope had been lit in our hearts
by my father who kept whispering, "There is hope, do not
despair. We will survive them."

We shared our hiding place with our closest friends and a
few neighbours. At around 10 o'clock at night on August
21, 1944, we were all seated around the table, trying to
gather strength for the next day. Suddenly, I heard
someone panting on the stairs. For a minute, we stopped
talking and did not breathe. Who was coming now?
My friend Chanale burst into the room. She had heard
about the slaughter on our street, so she came running.
She called my name but nobody came to the window.
She thought we were gone. I went downstairs with her,
happy that we had another evening together. We hardly
spoke. Somehow we knew it was our last time together.
It was late. We hugged each other but we did not say
goodbye. We did not want this to be our final parting.

*We wanted to hang on to something, hoping that another day would be ours.*

*The Germans surrounded our house the next day, on Tuesday August 22, 1944. They found us. Not a word was spoken, and not a tear was shed. After ten days of constant tension, we were almost relieved. We took our knapsacks, filled with a few precious belongings including my diary, some photos and some warm clothing. We went downstairs and were marched off by German soldiers to the gathering place. Thousands of ghetto dwellers were already here. We were then taken to the train station and loaded into cattle cars.*

*I have this picture stored away in my memory: The suffocating heat of the sealed wagon, bodies pressed together, the train stopping at a station. My father is standing on someone's shoulders in order to reach the tiny, barred window. His white hands are waving like flags in surrender, and his voice calls out to somebody at the station, "Where are we going?" He turns to us and all I see is the despair in his eyes as he reports, "They say the train is going to Auschwitz." I learned after the war that Chanale had died of typhus in Bergen-Belsen, the camp where I was liberated, just hours before the end of the war.*

## IN THE CONCENTRATION CAMPS

**Auschwitz was a deathcamp where people were gassed and** burned, while Bergen-Belsen was a concentration camp with abysmal conditions. I was in those camps. They are black holes in my memory, places into which I do not like to descend. I am afraid of the horrors hidden there, always ready to jump at me and rob me of peace and contentment.

Auschwitz was like a madhouse. Upon our arrival, we were thrown out from the cattle cars and immediately surrounded by SS-men with huge dogs and people in striped clothing. They were the Jews who worked at the train station. We were not allowed to take anything with us. The men were separated from the women. My father was taken from us and pushed to an area where the men were. We were then kicked into rows as an SS officer walked past, indicating with his thumb whether a person should go to the right or to the left. We did not know at the time that this SS officer was the infamous Dr. Mengele, known as the Angel of Death, and that going to the left meant going to the gas chambers, and to the right meant going to work camps. The women who went to the right, including myself, were taken into a room. Here our hair was shaved off and everything was taken from us, even our names. We were given numbers, marched naked in rows of five to a shower area, and given ill-fitting dresses and shoes. After the shower, we were led to a field surrounded by electric wires to spend the night. It was cold, wet, and scary. Out of nowhere, women appeared who were old inmates of Auschwitz. They had heard that a transport of women from Lodz had arrived and were looking for their loved ones. They whispered to us that we should try to enlist for work as soon as possible in order to get away from Auschwitz, because Auschwitz was hell.

The next morning, we were taken to empty barracks with cold cement floors on which we were to sleep. Every dawn, the SS made us stand outside in orderly rows for endless hours of roll-call. They counted us over and over again, while they screamed, shoved and hit us. We stood this way, in rows of five, for most of the day. Towards the evening, each group of five received a canteen of soup which we then shared by taking turns sipping it, as we had no spoons.

Some days later, we heard that they were signing up women for work at another camp. We rushed to sign up. Five hundred women, all from the Lodz Ghetto, were taken to a small camp, in a place called Sasel, near the port city of Hamburg. There we were to build pre-fabricated houses for bombed-out Germans. After Auschwitz, this was like paradise. No gas chambers, no chimneys, and no vicious dogs to chase us. It was still a concentration camp, we were still inmates, the SS could still do with us what they wanted, but we were able to work and we dared to hope that perhaps here we had a better chance of survival. Once again, we could call our mother "mother," without the fear that she might be taken away from us, a fear that was constantly with us at Auschwitz. The Nazis enjoyed tearing families apart. Here we had bunk beds and blankets instead of cement floors to sleep on, unlike in Auschwitz. We were lucky that we were put into a small barrack with only thirteen women. We soon became like one family, listening to each other's grief. One of the women in our barrack became the cook for the camp's SS guards. From time to time, she would smuggle leftovers into the barrack, hand them over to my mother who, as the oldest, most respected and loved in our barrack, would divide them equally.

A piercing whistle at dawn was our wake-up call. We would

quickly get ready for the roll-call, while assigned people would rush out to get the watery coffee and the daily bread ration for the rest of us. After roll-call, we were marched off to our work place, which was quite a distance away. I remember passing houses inhabited by Germans with curtained windows. I remember imagining the peaceful life behind those curtains. Perhaps children were getting ready for school, perhaps a father was going off to work, or perhaps there was a table with lots of food on it. It brought back the longing for my own warm, loving home.

We were in Sasel between October 1944 and March 1945. The days were long, the work was hard, and the weather wet, cold and miserable. At the end of the day, we would line up again to be marched back to the camp where the SS searched us. We were not allowed to bring anything back into the camp, not even a scrap of paper. After the search we had to line up in an orderly fashion for the watery soup, which was our evening meal. Soon after the meal, lights were put out, signalling the end of another day.

One evening during the search, potato peelings were found hidden in the clothes of two girls. We were all forced to line up again, handed sticks, and told that we would not receive our soup and would not be allowed back into the barracks unless each of us whipped the two girls. There were five hundred of us in the camp and not a single woman moved to lift a hand. We were beaten and threatened. However, nothing moved us to carry out the SS-men's orders. They brought pots of steaming soup into the yard and dumped them in the snow before our eyes. We stood outside, frozen and hungry, all through the night. In the morning, we were marched off to work without our bread ration. To this day, I am puzzled by our spontaneous behaviour, by this expression of solidarity towards our own, and by the fact that we were not more harshly punished for it.

Two people in particular left an imprint on my memory from that period. One is Herr Herbert, a German in his mid-forties. He was one of the overseers at our workplace and befriended us almost as soon as we arrived. I do not know what drew his attention to us. Perhaps my mother. Perhaps he noticed our care and love for each other. His friendliness and kindness restored our belief in human goodness and gave us hope. He would bring us little things from his wife almost every day, little items that made us feel human. Things like decent underwear, a warm flannel dressing-gown for my mother to wear under her thin coat, warm gloves, or tiny sandwiches. Herr Herbert would hide potatoes for us that he had stolen from the rations intended for the German workers. We would sneak these into the camp a few potatoes at a time, despite our knowledge of the great risk. We would eat them raw with our daily bread ration to fill our stomachs. At times, he would bring us a German newspaper feeding our hope about Nazi Germany's defeats. Herr Herbert used to call me "Sonia-Henie," after the famous skater. On November 3, 1944, my eighteenth birthday, I became ill with a blood infection and was allowed to stay in the camp for a day. When Herr Herbert did not see me at work, he asked my mother what had happened. My mother told him that I was sick and that today was my birthday. At the end of the day, Herr Herbert brought my mother three tiny apples to celebrate my birthday, which she then smuggled into the camp. This was, indeed, a precious gift, as we had forgotten both the taste of apples and the taste of human kindness.

Herr Herbert told us that he had a brother in Canada, and that he hoped to go there with his family after the war. At that time, Canada was like the name of a distant planet for us. I do not know what happened to Herr Herbert. He never told us his family name or where he lived. I think he felt it safer that way. We did not know where to look for him after the war to thank him for his humanity, for his goodness and decency. I am not sure if he realized that he had become a spark of hope for us, which sustained us during the morbid months ahead. I have never forgotten him.

The other person I remember from this period is Heltzia Dubner. She was my Latin teacher for the short time I had attended high school. She, too, was in Sasel, and we recognized one another when we met soon after our arrival. At the time, she was in her thirties. She was alone, having lost her family during a selection in Auschwitz. We became her family. My mother, with her unique way of embracing people and expressing her love and warmth, took Heltzia under her wing. We did not work on Sundays, which were spent washing, mending, and cleaning the barrack for inspection by the SS-women. However, later in the day, Heltzia would come by and, sitting on an upper bunk, tell us of her travels around the world. She charmed us and made the barrack walls disappear as she took us along on those journeys. She was such a wonderful story-teller. I was enchanted by her stories about Paris, and it was then that I made a second promise to myself. I decided that if I survived, I would go to Paris and, if possible, live there, at least for a while. Heltzia Dubner survived and lived in Sweden after the war. She passed away some years ago.

The first few months of 1945 were marked in Sasel by frequent air-raid sirens. They were a signal for the Germans to go into their bomb shelters. The SS were openly horrified by the sirens, which were like music to our ears. The SS would hide, but we would go out into the open to shout and sing and wave to the Allied airplanes bombing Nazi Germany. We began to realize that the end was not far and prayed that we would be able to wait it out in Sasel where we had a chance to survive. However, this was not to be.

In early March, we were marched out of the camp, forced into cattle cars once again, and shuttled back and forth for three days. We did not know where we were headed, and judging by their surprised faces, it seemed that the SS guards did not know either. Outside, spring was in the air. The guards allowed us to keep the door of the cattle car open. We could smell the clean air and see the budding trees. Somehow, we did not abandon hope on this journey until the train stopped and we began to march towards the gate of another camp, Bergen-Belsen. We were pushed into a huge empty barrack. Outside, we could see mountains of corpses. There was no water, no food, no work; only endless roll-calls. Was this the end? It seemed as though there was nothing else to do here but to die. However, my mother did not allow us to give up. She kept telling us to hang on a while longer, just a while longer. We were not aware of days or dates.

One day, we noticed that there were no more roll-calls, and that the guards outside the barracks were wearing white armbands. However, they were still shooting at us at random. We did not understand the meaning of the white armbands. We thought they meant that the guards had surrendered, and therefore could not understand why they continued to shoot. We were afraid to leave the barrack because of the shooting. Besides, we were too weak to move. Suddenly, one early morning, someone banged on the door and we heard voices shouting in Polish, "Open up, we are free, free, free!" We did not believe it. We could not imagine that this could be true. Could this be freedom? If it was, we had no strength to rejoice. Someone slowly opened the bolted door. Standing there were British soldiers, tears streaming from their eyes, overwhelmed by what they saw in Bergen-Belsen. We were later told that this day was April 15, 1945. We were liberated.

✻ ✻ ✻

The first thought that came to my mind was about my father. Could he be somewhere in the same camp? Perhaps he, too, had survived. Suddenly, we were in a hurry to become stronger. We had to look for him.

The first thing the British soldiers did was pipe fresh water into the camp. They then began distributing cans of rich, fat foods. Unfortunately, the food was too rich for our shrivelled stomachs. My mother, in her wisdom, did not allow us to eat this food. Indeed, many people died because of it. Instead, she got a few potatoes and boiled them in clean water on a fire that she had made outside. We were soon transferred to another camp, also in Bergen-Belsen. However, it was not a concentration camp. Rather, it had been used as a camp for the Hitler Youth organization. We were put in houses with nice rooms, comfortable bunk beds, enough blankets to keep us warm, and sheets and pillows. It was a real luxury!

However, my sister Chava became sick with typhus and our hearts were heavy with fear and worry. Luckily, teams of doctors from all over Europe were already at work here, saving as many lives as they could, and Chava soon recovered. It was the beginning of summer. Our hair had begun growing back. Our bodies were filling out slowly. British soldiers would sometimes whistle at us as they passed by and call me "Gingy" because of my red hair. I liked it. I liked the colour of my growing hair. I liked being alive. The summer was beautiful that year.

# RETURN TO LIFE, IN SEARCH OF FATHER

Only when I myself became a mother did it dawn on me that my mother, and mothers in general, experienced the horrors of the war much more deeply than those of us who were younger. My sister Chava and I were able to escape into books, relationships, and involvements with friends and with the movement. But for my mother, our survival was an ongoing, everpresent concern. I also understood that her constant love and care were what sustained us. She nurtured us with her constant encouragement, and her constant watching over us. As long as she was around, we were a family and had to survive in order not to cause her pain. We never talked about Tate, my father. It was too painful. We did not dare to hope aloud that fate would single us out and restore my father to us. However, each of us secretly hoped for it.

After Chava's recovery from typhus in Bergen-Belsen, our thoughts returned to my father. There were only women in the part of the camp where we lived. Slowly, as if from nowhere, men began to appear. They came from all over Germany in search of their loved ones: mothers, sisters, wives, daughters, and sweethearts. Committees were formed in all of the camps for displaced persons, to organize camp life and compile lists of survivors for circulation in other camps.

One Friday night, at an *oyneg-Shabbes*, or gathering to celebrate the Sabbath, Chava and I noticed a man standing at the centre of the field where the dinner was taking place. He was surrounded by women calling out the names of the men for whom they were looking. We approached the group and immediately recognized our cousin Aryeh, who now lives in Tel Aviv. We called out his name. He looked at us for a second and then he ran to us, hugged and kissed us, and began to cry. Everyone around us was crying. People thought we were embracing our Tate. Then, someone rushed to my mother to bring her the unbelievable news that the miracle happened: our Tate had survived. When we got back to our room with Aryeh, she was shaking and crying, as she stood in the middle of the room, unable to move. But she soon understood what had happened. Aryeh was looking for his wife and two daughters. They did not survive.

More men came to Bergen-Belsen. Like all the other women looking for their loved ones, we went to the entrance gate of the camp every day to call out our father's name. We hoped that someone among them would have known or seen him, or at least would have recognized his name. And, indeed, one day a man approached us, asking us if we were looking for Avrom Rosenfarb, the one who had worked at the co-operative store in the ghetto. He knew Tate and had seen him two days before the end of the war, so we thought surely he would be alive somewhere, perhaps in a hospital. We ran back to our mother, shouting the entire way, "Ta is alive! He lives! He is alive!"

We decided that mother would remain at Bergen-Belsen in case my father came looking for us, and that Chava and I would set out to look for him. We were prepared to look for him in every German town, city and village. We did not have much to wear except a jacket and skirt my mother had made for us from an old blue camp blanket.

At that time, the roads in Germany were not yet open for civilian traffic. We were told by the Bergen-Belsen Jewish Committee that we would have to find transportation ourselves. This meant mainly hitchhiking. We were also informed that all of Germany was under curfew, and that people were not allowed to walk or travel at night. We were told that in most cities, there were Jewish committees that would provide us with shelter for the night, but that in smaller towns we would have to contact the mayor for assistance in finding shelter in a German home. And so, we set out with hope in our hearts, but with apprehension about the unknown. We took some cans of food and cartons of cigarettes for the journey. We had no money, but cigarettes were a good trading commodity for whatever we might need on the road.

During the journey, I saw black people for the first time. They were American soldiers. Until then, I had only seen black people in the circus in Poland. Chava and I both started smoking. We were at times frustrated and upset when we would stand for hours with our thumbs out and no vehicle would stop for us, or when we could not find shelter for a night and we feared that we would have to spend the night on the street. It never happened though. At the last minute someone would open a door and provide us with a bed.

At that time, it seemed as though everyone in Germany was on the road: German refugees returning from somewhere, concentration camp survivors — some still in the striped camp garments — trying to get out of Germany. Sometimes we saw groups of unarmed German soldiers being detained by Allied patrons trying to determine whether or not they were in fact disguised SS-men. We hitch-hiked from one city to another in the direction of Munich and Feldafing, a large nearby camp for displaced persons.

At times, we had to find shelter for the night ourselves, especially in the small towns and villages where there was no Jewish committee or no mayor to find it for us. We would knock on the doors of sleeping homes until someone would let us in and allow us to stay overnight. I remember one such home well. We were in a small hole of a town, tired and already desperate, for it seemed as though no one was willing to let us in. However, one door finally opened and a young woman let us in. We told her who we were and our destination. She did not say much except that she did not know anything about the things we were telling her, that her husband had not come back from the war, and that she had two small children. She took us to the room that was to be ours for the night. It had a large bed with huge white pillows, clean white sheets, and warm blankets. We peered into the big, heavy wardrobe in the room full of clothing. We picked two white kerchiefs, one for Chava and one for myself. The next morning, we got up early and placed ourselves, thumbs out, on the road. We pushed onward, in jeeps, trucks, and even once in a large truck with horses.

Our first stop in each town and city was the Jewish Com-mittee, if there was one, to read the lists of survivors' names. Our next stop was usually at the local hospitals to check the lists of the sick. In one hospital, I do not recall where, we found a person with my father's name, Avrom Rosenfarb. I remember my heart pounding upon seeing my father's name, and then my overwhelming sadness upon discovering that the man was not my father.

In the German city of Frankfurt, we were told by someone at the Jewish Committee that there would be a train leaving for Munich. We were told to head to the outskirts of the city where the train would stop. When we arrived, an American soldier was there on guard. We did our best to explain in German, as Chava and I knew no English, who we were, and where we wanted to go. He understood, and we could see how upset he was with our story. He promised to stop the train for us, but made us understand that it would be a freight train because passenger trains were not running yet. In the meantime, he gave us chocolate and fruit and his address in America, in case we ever came there.

The American soldier stopped the train headed for Munich, our destination. It was packed with loose coal. He helped us climb onto the pile. There were people already sitting on the coal who had climbed on at other points along the rails. It was not a very com-fortable ride, yet we were happy to sit on the coal knowing that the next day we would be in Munich. We had no blankets, and it was raining, but someone shared a blanket with us. People were telling each other their stories — they were so familiar to us. Everyone was looking for a loved one. Not everyone on the train was Jewish. I do not know who they were, but it did not matter at the time. We felt a kinship with them — they were as homeless as we were. Slowly, night gave way to day. At one point, Chava and I looked at each other and started to laugh uncontrollably. We were both completely blue. The suits our mother had made for us were not colourfast, and in the rain every piece of our exposed skin turned blue. What a sight. Finally, we arrived in Munich where we were told that we would have to take a train to the Feldafing displaced persons (DP) camp. But first we had to find a water pump where we could wash the blue dye off our skin so as not to shock people.

## FELDAFING

**We reached Feldafing sensing that in all probability, our father did not survive.** We met some Bundists at the camp, who had already established contacts all over Germany in an effort to find Bundist survivors. They told us that our father had been in the Dachau concentration camp. When the Germans discovered that the Americans were approaching, they put all the camp inmates on trains to transport them somewhere. We learned that American airplanes bombarded the trains and many inmates were killed, including my father. The Americans must have thought that they were military trains. Our Bundist friends surrounded us with love and care, and tried as best they could to soothe our pain. Among those Bundists was Zalmenke. He became our friend until the end of his life. He lived in New York, but came to visit with us years later in Canada, to warm himself at our family fire. He loved us all dearly. In his pocket, he always carried a faded picture of his wife and two little girls who had perished. We loved his visits, as we loved him.

The group of Bundists became like an extended family to us, and we decided to bring our mother to Feldafing. Once we had returned with our mother, our friends organized a lavish party to celebrate my nineteenth birthday. It was the first celebration for all of us, and as the youngest among them, my birthday was a good excuse for a party. There was a lot of singing, eating, and drinking. Someone even baked a cake for the occasion.

Eventually, hope returned to our hearts as we started to plan our future. Chava and I wanted to return to Poland and to go back to school. We heard that schools were now free there. Besides, Poland was where we had come from, and it seemed logical to us to return there, as we had nowhere else to go. People were returning home, to France, Belgium, and Holland, but my mother did not want to go back. We had nobody to whom to return, she kept telling us. Poland, the country of our birth, was not friendly to us Jews.

At that time, Bundist groups in the United States and Canada began sending money to Bundist groups in the displaced persons camps and throughout Europe to help their members start anew. We really had to start from scratch. We wore clothes donated by people from the United States, ugly clothes. We longed for a normal life, a normal home, and decent clothing. We wanted to leave Germany — fast. The Bundist leadership in Feldafing received money from the Bund in America to arrange for smugglers to take groups of Bundists across the border to Belgium. In Brussels, local Bundists received them and helped to legalize their status. We left with a group of eight women, and were the second group to leave this way. We had no luggage, but our hearts were full of hope, and our heads were full of dreams. However, when we reached the Belgian border, the smuggler decided that he did not want to risk imprisonment and left us literally in the middle of nowhere. In front of us was the Belgian border, behind us, Germany, and we were in the middle. Prior to our departure, it had been decided that, once safe on the Belgian side, we would give the smuggler a note, the text of which had been worked out with our friends in Feldafing, informing them that the smuggler had done his job. The German smuggler demanded the note from us, even though he had not taken us across. We advised our friends in a coded language that the smuggler had abandoned us and that they should not to pay him or use him again. Meanwhile, we were in no man's land — no longer in Germany and not yet in Belgium.

54

It was late at night, an unfriendly moonless night. We did not know what to do, whether to go back or to move on. In the distance, we saw what looked like a light in a window. Slowly we approached it. We thought the light was coming from a house still on the German side. The group decided that when were near the house, Chava would knock on the door. The rest of us would hide behind the trees outside. Chava knocked on the door and it opened. We saw a woman in the doorway and could hear Chava telling her that she was a former inmate of a concentration camp, and that she wanted to get to Brussels. She asked if the woman could help her. Our hearts pounding, we heard the woman respond, "Ya." Chava thanked her profusely and then told her she was not alone but with her family, seven people, and that we all wanted to go to Brussels because we had relatives there. Chava asked whether we could come in. The woman opened the door for us, and we entered with a sigh of relief. She put food and a warm drink on the table. There was also a man in the room. We told them about our unsuccessful attempt to cross the border. I do not know whether the people in the house were themselves smugglers, or whether they just decided to help us, especially since we told them that they would be handsomely rewarded if they brought us to Brussels. We stayed overnight in the friendly house.

Early the next morning, we were told to board a school bus that was waiting in front of the house. We got in and were instructed to lie flat on the floor. After a short ride, the man driving the bus told us that we were in Belgium. Two taxis were already waiting to take us to Brussels. We knew the address of the Bund and the Workmen's Circle[12] in Brussels by heart. It was early evening when the taxis stopped in front of the house on Rue de Goujon where the Workmen's Circle was located. The Bundist members of Brussels had been ex-

---

12 The Workmen's Circle was a Bundist mutual aid association. For more, see Glossary.

pecting us, although they were unaware of our mishap. Our friends from Feldafing, who had made the crossing with the group had left before us, were there too. The group after us had been arrested and put in a Belgian jail for a while. There was hugging and kissing, laughter and tears. We had made it. The smugglers received their reward, and before they left, they were invited to join us for dinner. They could hardly believe that the people who paid for our crossing and received us were not family, but rather people whom we had just met for the very first time. And we could hardly believe our good fortune ourselves. We were out of Germany and out of the camps. We were truly "free at last." It was October 1945.

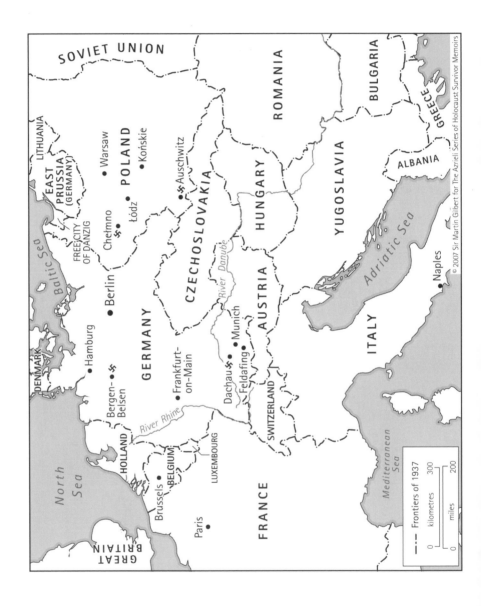

Henia's sister Chava, father Avrom Rosenfarb, Henia, mother Simma (Poland, 1927). This is the only surviving photograph of Henia's father.

Henia's Aunt Tziotzia (bottom left) and her family (Poland, early 1930s).

Bundist demonstration, Henia (far right) (Brussels, c. 1948).

Henia (right) with friends at a Bundist camp (Brussels, 1948).

Henia's mother Simma (Belgium, late 1940s).

60

Bono Wiener, Bundist Activist
(Poland, date unknown).

Henia's sister Chava, Chava's husband
Henry Morgentaler, Henia's mother Simma,
and Henia in Brussels (late 1940s).

Henia and her best friend Krysia (Paris, c. 1948).

Henia (Brussels, c. 1948).    Nochem Reinhartz (Paris, c. 1948).

Henia (Brussels, c. 1948).

62

△ Henia's sister Chava Rosenfarb.
◁ Henia and Nochem (North of Toronto, c. 1951).

Henia and Nochem (Toronto, 1951).

Henia's Mother Simma Rosenfarb and Henia's daugther Adele (Toronto, 1953).

Henia and daughter Adele (Toronto, 1953).

Henia and her best friend Krysia (Toronto, 1980s).

Henia's son, Avrom or 'Bamie', Henia, her daughter Adele, and Nochem at
Adele's wedding (Toronto, 1980).

Can you imagine how it feels to be set loose in a beautiful city like Brussels after years of being enclosed in a ghetto and in the camps? We did not know what to do first. Chava, my mother and I were still dressed in the clothes that we had received in the displaced persons camps: yellow shoes, green socks, and blue coats. They were all gifts from American Jewry. In our attire, we stood out among the nicely dressed local population. But we did not care. And yet, out of habit, we still looked behind us from time to time to make sure no German soldiers were following us. Our first few days in Brussels were spent in a department store going up and down the escalator, laughing loudly and beaming with delight. We had never seen anything like it before. We also spent one day going from one moviehouse to another. Not that we understood what the films were about, since we did not know any French then, but we had not been to the movies in six years.

Soon, however, we had to begin thinking about a place to live and about work. We had been staying with a Bundist family. However, we did not want to be dependent upon the handouts of Jewish organizations. We wanted finally to get rid of our yellow shoes, to buy our own shoes, and whatever else we needed. But what kind of work could we do? We had no skills. During the war years, Chava and I had dreamt about continuing our education, should we survive the war. However, that seemed impossible as we did not know any French, the language spoken in Brussels. Besides, we had to earn a living.

Therefore, we decided to learn a trade. Chava and I registered at a vocational school to learn dressmaking. It was run by the Organization for Rehabilitation and Training, or ORT, a charitable society that provides training in trades for Jews around the world. As concentration camp survivors, we were able to attend the school for free, and were even given pocket money. However, after a short time, we realized that we could not follow the discipline demanded in a school setting, such as being required to raise our hands when we wanted to say something, or ask permission to use the washroom. These are important rules to follow in school, but we felt that we were just too old for this. Besides, after all the forced obedience during the war years, we did not want to have to be obedient again. So we left.

At that time, some refugees opened workshops in their homes, taking on work from factories, mainly in the garment industry. I began working in such a home workshop, learning to finish garments by hand. I went from place to place, wherever people were willing to teach me, and also willing to pay a small salary, until I became quite skilled. Finally, I found a good place to work, not far from where we lived. The people for whom I worked were extremely nice, childless concentration camp survivors. They treated me like a member of the family. There were also some other people working there. I worked twelve hours a day, from eight o'clock in the morning until eight o'clock at night, with one hour for lunch, which I ate at home. On Saturdays, I worked until two o'clock in the afternoon. I was paid well, and on Saturdays, I would buy *nasheray*, or snacks, like chocolate and halvah, to bring home, along with money in my pocket. I gave my earnings to my mother, and she would give me pocket money for all my needs.

I was also teaching Yiddish at the Workmen's Circle school three times a week. I went from work to school and came back later to finish my day's work twice a week, and taught classes on Sunday mornings as well. This was the beginning of my teaching career, and a way in which I could earn money and fulfill the promise I had made to myself during the war years. I loved Brussels and although life was hard, I was young and apprently pretty. I loved living.

Our circle of friends grew continuously. Many Polish Jews who had spent the war in concentration camps or in Russia streamed into Belgium. The Workmen's Circle in Brussels was one of the places where we gathered. We joined the Brussels Bundist group, where we organized a sports club modelled after *Morgenshtern*, the one in pre-war Poland. I was also a member of a drama club that performed plays. We organized summer camps in the Belgian countryside, or near the sea. Once we organized an international camp for young Bundists from London, Paris, and Brussels. What a summer that was. I made lifelong friends among those campers. It seemed to us that the world was ours to explore. I worked, and eventually my mother could afford to move into a small, but very pleasant apartment not far from the Workmen's Circle. By then, Chava was married and living nearby.

It was at this time that my good friend Krysia came into my life. For my twentieth birthday, Krysia bought me one shoe of a pair that we used to admire in a store window, but which I could not afford to buy. I bought the second shoe myself. They were my very first pair of beautiful beige suede shoes.

Soon after, I took my first trip to Paris. I already had friends there, whom I had met at one of our Bundist-run summer camps. The first Socialist International youth conference took place in Paris after the war, and the Belgian Bund youth movement sent me and two boys as delegates. We had no visas to enter France, since at that time refugees were unable to obtain visas. However, we were instructed on how we could smuggle ourselves into the city of Lille, in France. From there, we took the train to Paris. I was finally in the city of my dreams. I immediately fell in love with Paris, and stayed for two weeks with a friend.

When I returned to Belgium, I began to contemplate how

I could fulfill the second promise that I had made to myself — to live in Paris — when an opportunity presented itself. I was told that there was a teachers' college that trained Hebrew and Yiddish teachers in a three-year course. It seemed made for me. I could receive a teaching certificate and become a trained teacher in Paris.

I wrote a letter to the school expressing my desire to be accepted and telling them about myself, including the reasons why I wanted to attend the school and become a Yiddish teacher. A few days later, I was invited for an interview. I was very excited but also apprehensive. I was worried about how I would get to Paris this time. I already knew that as a refugee, I could not leave Belgium, as I would not be allowed back. There was only one way to get there — the same way as before, but I had to do it all by myself.

Dressed in my best clothing, I made my way to Paris, had my interview, and was accepted. The school even agreed to let me complete the course in two years, instead of the usual three. When I returned to Brussels, I had to work out a way to move to Paris legally. I do not remember what time of the year it was, but the older students from the Brussels Workmen's Circle School were going to Paris as well. The principal knew about my plans, and it was decided that, along with two other teachers, I would officially accompany the students to Paris, and then I would remain there. The school in Paris agreed to arrange my student visa. My friends in Paris rented a tiny room for me in a rundown hotel where some of my friends were already living. I received a small scholarship established by a Belgian Bundist family intended for young refugees who wanted to further their education. The Workmen's Circle School in Paris offered me a class to teach, which provided me with the means to support myself. My mother wholeheartedly endorsed my project, and was as enthusiastic about it as I was. Still, I knew how difficult it would be for her to part with me. How generous my mother was with her love for me.

PARIS

The Hôtel Côte d'Or was well-located, close to a Metro station
and to the centre of the city. My tiny room had a bed from which
I could reach the sink and the window on one side, with a small
table and the entrance door on the other. There was a small closet
for my clothes, with a drawer at the bottom for food. Food was still
rationed at that time but I had enough for my needs. I made my
tiny room comfortable and cosy and felt very much at home. I
began classes and became acquainted with my colleagues and
teachers. The students were all young survivors, and the teachers
were well-known scholars in their fields. By that time, my French
was already quite good. Paris was full of music, theatre, art and fun.
I took it all in with joy. I was on top of the world and felt extremely
fortunate. I was in Paris and I was studying. I also taught at the
Workmen's Circle school three times a week. On weekends, I went
out with my young Bundist friends to the theatre, or just for walks
on the boulevards that were always full of people.

From time to time I would go home to Brussels to see my
family and friends. By then, I was already an expert in crossing the
border illegally. My friend Krysia would come to visit the same illegal
way. One such visit stands out in my memory. Krysia came to spend
New Year's Eve with my friends and me, and stayed at my place. I still
had classes that day and as I was getting ready to leave for school, I
heard a commotion in the hallway. I went out and saw a policeman at
the end of the hall. I knew what was happening. Police were frequent

visitors at the hotels and other places where refugees lived. They would check whether the tenants had permits to live in Paris, as the city was full of illegal immigrants at that time. I was not afraid because not only did I have a permit to live in France, but I had an identity card that stated that I was a *"Professeur en langue Yidiche."* The police respected the title tremendously. But Krysia was visiting illegally, and if caught, could have been sent to jail. I went back to the room, told Krysia to get dressed quickly and hide under the bed. I made the bed as neatly as I could, and when I heard the superintendent near my door, I opened it wide. With my briefcase and identity card in hand, a broad smile on my face, and the nicest "Bonjour Madame" I could muster, I ran down the stairs. I did not like that superintendent, as she used to steal the chocolate and coffee from the food parcels my mother sent to me, so it felt good to trick her. I did not go to school that day. Instead, I waited across the street in a coffeehouse until I saw the police leave the hotel. Krysia came out from under the bed, and we then went for a walk through the streets of Paris. We were in a joyous mood; laughing, giggling and being silly, pleased with ourselves for fooling the police. On one of the elegant streets, we passed a store window with a display of beautiful photographs. We stopped to admire the pictures and at the same time, had a splendid idea. Why not have our picture taken right then and there, so that we could one day show our grandchildren what we looked like when we were young. It cost us a fortune, but we were pleased. The photographs came out beautifully, and we promised ourselves that we would display them in our homes, wherever we might live. And this we did.

Paris was called the City of Light, not only because of its beauty, but also because it was a city that always made room for refugees, for those who were oppressed and persecuted in their home countries. It was a city rich in all forms of art even then, so soon after the war. It was in Paris that I learned to love beautiful music and theatre, and to appreciate paintings. I was a frequent visitor to the Louvre, and I became familiar with the names and paintings of the masters. I saw the paintings of Marc Chagall and Vincent Van Gogh for the first time, and fell in love with them. Paris was alive with interesting people and places, and I wanted to meet and see them all. Once, while sitting with my friends at a lecture given by a Yiddish writer, I felt someone yanking my hair from behind. I turned around and saw the grinning face of a young man whom I had met at a Bundist gathering. I could not interrupt the lecture, so I did not say anything, but I was so angry. After the lecture, I went over to him and asked in a loud angry voice, "Why did you pull my hair? Don't you have anything else to do?" "Oh well, I could not help myself, your hair wanted to be pulled," he replied. This was Nochem, the man I would later marry.

After Chava left for Canada with her husband Henry, my mother came to live with me in Paris. She also came illegally. The Workmen's Circle in Paris arranged a permit to legalize her stay. In anticipation of my mother's arrival, I moved to a larger room, one floor up, on the fourth floor. I bought a small kerosene stove, a few pots and dishes, and we were ready for housekeeping. I knew that my mother would not like to eat out the way I did, and besides, we had very little money. We also expected that within a year of Chava's departure, we, too, would leave for Canada. As soon as Chava arrived in Canada, she began applying for the papers that would allow us to immigrate there. At that time, many of our friends had already left Europe. Some went to the United States, some to Canada, and others to Australia. My future husband Nochem left for Canada in 1949.

I continued with my classes, and was chosen as the valedictorian of my graduating class. This was an important event for me. Not only had I fulfilled both of the promises that I had made to myself, but now I was a Yiddish teacher with a diploma. I felt that this would enable me to teach wherever there were Yiddish schools. Many famous Yiddish writers from the United States and Europe came to participate in this first graduation at the school. We were the first post-war professionally-trained Yiddish and Hebrew teachers. The hall was packed. My mother sat in the first row, beaming. I wore a new dress for the occasion. Krysia's mother and stepfather, who lived at that time in Paris, came as well. Her stepfather often traveled to the United States on business, and returned from one of his trips with a beautiful navy dress for me. I wore this same dress to my wedding and to all the celebrations connected with it.

My mother felt comfortable in Paris with my friends in our tiny and not-so-comfortable lodgings. She never complained. My friends adored her, and for me, this was a golden opportunity to get to know her not only as my mother, but also as a woman, as a person, and as a friend. I always had so many questions for her about her childhood and her many siblings, some in Lodz, and some in Argentina. I asked her about my father and how they had met. My mother enjoyed sharing her past with me. A strong bond formed between us.

I spent the summer of 1950 working as a counsellor at a camp for Jewish children, many of whom had been orphaned by the war. The camp was named Ika Haym, after a Jewish woman and resistance fighter who was killed by the Germans. I was permitted to bring my mother with me, and it was there, on 8 August, that we received a telegram that Chava had given birth to a little girl named Goldie, after her husband Henry's mother. This was my mother's first grandchild, and my first niece. I was overjoyed. However, my mother's joy was mixed with tears, which at the time I could not understand. To celebrate, I prepared a party for the staff. I bought wine, and the camp's cook prepared sandwiches and cookies. Everyone attended the party, except my mother.

"Forgive me, child," she said to me. "You go and sing and dance. There is a lot to be happy about. We truly survived, but I will stay here for now."

"But why?" I kept asking her. The party was for her in celebration of her first grandchild. But she did not join us that evening.

Only years later, when I myself became a grandmother and was able to hold my newborn grandchildren, did I understand her sadness. She needed to be near her daughter, to hold her first newborn grandchild in her arms. And perhaps the tears had been for her husband, my father, who was not there to share in this miracle with her, and the significance it carried for the continuation of our family.

The necessary papers from Canada arrived, and my mother and I prepared to leave Europe. We were to travel by boat, as few people, and certainly not refugees, travelled by airplane. All of our travel expenses were paid for by the American Joint Distribution Committee (JDC), a Jewish organization in the United States that helps Jewish refugees. Prior to receiving our entrance visa to Canada, we had to pass a medical examination and interviews at the Canadian embassy. We successfully passed all requirements, and were to leave Paris at the beginning of January 1951. I had tearful partings with my friends, my students, and the teachers at the school where I worked. I still have a picture that was taken at the party on this occasion. In it, I look solemn and sad, surrounded by the children I so loved. I maintained correspondence with some of them for many years after.

## ON THE BOAT

We left Paris in the beginning of January 1951. Our precious possessions consisted of a trunk, which I still have, filled with books, and a few suitcases. We left early in the morning. It was still dark and rainy, which reflected my mood. The train took us from Paris to Naples, Italy. There, we boarded the boat to make the Atlantic crossing. Until the boat arrived, we stayed in the big hall of a building along with hundreds of people, all refugees of different nationalities. Many of them were Jews. We were all to become *shifshvester un brider*, or boat sisters and brothers.

We waited for five days in Naples. Some went to see Pompeii, but we explored Naples as much as we could. The first day we went out, I noticed people were staring at me, pointing their fingers, and laughing. I asked my mother whether my face or clothes were clean. I did not understand what was going on until I heard people saying in a mocking tone "pantalone," and something else, which I did not understand. I knew that "pantalone" meant pants, like in French. I had been wearing black pants that a dear friend of ours made for me before we left Paris. I was also wearing a beautiful black windbreaker and black velvet beret that I had bought before the trip. I thought I looked really smart. So why were they laughing? I later learned that at the time, women in Italy did not wear pants. Therefore, the sight of a woman in pants was hilarious to them.

We were lucky that our ship *Nea Hellas*, a Greek steamer,

was a very elegant passenger ship. Many refugees, including my husband Nochem, made the voyage in freight boats. Our cabins were below deck, but very clean and comfortable. The meals were served by waiters wearing white gloves in a beautiful dining room on tables covered with white tablecloths. The steamer also carried private passengers but no distinction was made between the refugees and them, except for the location of the cabins. There was wine and music with every dinner and entertainment each night. It was fun, until some passengers became seasick. I felt fine, but my mother was very ill, and spent six days of the trip in the cabin. She stood near me on deck though one morning when we spotted land, the shores of Canada. We were approaching Halifax.

The train took us from Halifax to Montreal. It was a long journey. We were tired and apprehensive, but also excited about soon seeing my sister Chava and our little Goldie. We passed vast snow-covered spaces, and here and there a lonely house. No towns, no people, just emptiness. Was this what Canada was all about? We did not know. No one seemed to know. People did not say much. We sat quietly in our places, faces glued to the windows. A day passed, and then a night, and finally the fields began to disappear. The people on the train became animated. We were approaching Montreal. I stood at the open door of the train as we came into the station, and suddenly I heard someone shouting, "Mama! Mama!" Chava was there, meeting the train. Thanks to a friend of hers, Mr. Hershman, she received permission to come out onto the platform. The meeting was tearful, but these were tears of joy. We were together once again, and we could finally hold little Goldie in our hands. She was four months old, and was the first grandchild in our family. We lived with Chava, and, in a very loving way, she made us feel as though her home was also our home.

Life in Montreal was not easy for immigrants at that time. We came to this new country without a penny to our name, without any knowledge of English, or the customs of the land. I was luckier than some as I knew French, and I had my family and some friends who had come before us. Nochem was living with his parents in Toronto, and we saw each other often. I found a job in a French department store in Old Montreal, where I worked in the purse and gloves department. I was called "La Parisienne" in the store because the French I spoke from Paris was different from the French spoken in Montreal. I enjoyed working there since it provided me with the opportunity to meet people and talk to them. Friday afternoons, teenage girls would come straight from school to look at purses and try on gloves. In the evenings, working women would stop by my counter to try on scarves and look at other merchandise. The store was in a working-class district and sometimes people could afford only to look at the merchandise. The women liked to talk to me because they liked the way I spoke French, and I liked to talk to them, although it took me a while to understand their French. My wages were very low, so I soon started to look for work that paid better. I went to work in a factory that made children's clothing, and worked there until Nochem and I were married on March 8, 1952.

We had quite a few wedding celebrations. The one I liked best was in our home. Nochem's parents came from Toronto and all our friends came to celebrate with us. It was a joyous affair with lots of drinking, eating, singing and merry-making. Soon after, we left for Toronto. I did not enjoy Toronto at first. I missed my family very much, and the city seemed half-asleep to me compared to Montreal, which was so full of life. I knew French and therefore could communicate with people in Montreal. I had friends there. But in Toronto I had to learn a new language. I did not know anybody. The little houses with their gardens reminded me of a small town. On Sunday evenings, everything was closed — no restaurants, no movies, no theatres. I went to work at the Tip Top Tailors factory. My days were busy, but the evenings were long because my husband Nochem worked at night, and I missed my family terribly. But slowly, I became part of the Bundist group in Toronto. People were very warm, inviting us into their homes and into their lives. My family came to visit often, particularly my mother, who had old friends from Lodz in

Toronto. She would stay with us for long periods, and this was always a special time for us.

The birth of our children Adele and Avrom, was a most beautiful time in my life. I did not work anymore, and I loved being a mother. When my daughter Adele was one year old, we bought our first home at 261 Glenholme Avenue. My son Avrom was born there. We all loved this house. We were happy, as we had our own home, and felt that we had put down roots in our new country and in Toronto, which I increasingly began to like. Above all, we had our children. They seemed like a miracle to me. We spent many summers in the Laurentian Mountains near Montreal. My mother was still alive. She lived with Chava, and would spend the summers together with all of us. My husband Nochem would come for a couple of weeks during his holidays, and I would stay for the summer.

I took up teaching again when my son Avrom began kindergarten. I began teaching at the Workmen's Circle's Peretz School, and later, at the Bialik Hebrew Day School, both in Toronto. My days had their own rhythm of work and raising my children. I thought my children uniquely beautiful, and I am filled with pride to see them grow up to be the kind of people who they are.

These are the bits and pieces of my life.

# GLOSSARY

**Aktion (pl. Aktionen):** [German: action] The rounding up and deportation of targeted individuals and groups, most often for mass murder.

**Auschwitz:** German name for Oswiecim [Polish], a town in southern Poland approximately thirty-seven kilometres from Krakow; and the name of the largest complex of concentration camps, built nearby. The Auschwitz complex contained three main camps: Auschwitz I, a slave labour camp built in May 1940; Auschwitz-Birkenau, a deathcamp built in early 1942; and Auschwitz-Monowitz, a slave labour camp built in October 1942. In 1941 Auschwitz I was testing site for the use the lethal gas Zyklon B as a method of mass killing. The Auschwitz complex was liberated by the Soviet army in January 1945.

**Baluty:** Originally a town on the northern edge of Lodz where many Jews settled, due to residence restrictions; later incorporated into the city as a densely populated Jewish working-class district; the location of the Lodz Ghetto

**Bergen-Belsen:** Concentration camp established near Celle, Germany, in 1940, initially for prisoners of war. After 1943, it held "exchange" Jews, whom Germany hoped to use in peace negotiations with the Allies. After 1944, it held labourers and the ill who were left to die by starvation and disease. Towards the end of the war, prisoners from camps close to the front lines were taken there, primarily on death marches. British forces liberated the camp on 15 April 1945.

**Bund:** The *Algemeyner Yidisher Arbeter Bund in Lite, Poyln, un Rusland,* or the Jewish Workers' Alliance in Lithuania, Poland, and Russia. Founded in 1897 in Vilna, the Bund was a social-democratic revolutionary movement that fought for the rights of the Yiddish-speaking Jewish worker, advocated national cultural autonomy, and championed the Yiddish language and Yiddish secular culture. In interwar Poland, the Bund served as one of many Jewish political parties, with affiliated schools, youth groups, and sports clubs.

**Chelmno:** The first deathcamp, located sixty kilometres from Lodz, established on 8 December 1941. From January 1942 until March 1943, Jews were deported there from the Lodz Ghetto. Deportations resumed in June 1944 to facilitate the liquidation of the Lodz Ghetto. Victims were killed in vans, with exhaust fumes piped into the interior.

**Dachau:** The first concentration camp established in Nazi Germany, in March 1933 in the northern part of the town of Dachau; originally used as a camp for political prisoners, which included political opponents, Communists, Social Democrats, and trade unionists, as well as Jehovah's Witnesses and Roma. The number of Jews interned there rose considerably after Kristallnacht on 10 November 1938. The camp also functioned as a training centre for SS guards. In 1942, the crematorium area was constructed next to the main camp. By the spring of 1945, Dachau and its subcamps held more than 67,665 registered prisoners, 43,350 categorized as political prisoners, and 22,100 as Jews. As the American Allied forces neared the camp in April 1945, the Nazis forced 7,000 prisoners, primarily Jews, on a grueling death march to Tegernsee, another camp in southern Germany.

**Ghetto:** A confined residential area for Jews. The term originated in Venice, Italy in 1516, with a law requiring all Jews to live on a segregated, gated island known as Ghetto Nuovo. Throughout the Middle-Ages in Europe, Jews were often forcibly confined to gated Jewish neighborhoods. During the Holocaust, the Nazis forced Jews to live in crowded and unsanitary conditions in a dilapidated district of a city. Most ghettoes were enclosed by brick walls or wooden fences with barbed wire. The largest ghetto in German-occupied Poland was the Warsaw Ghetto; the Lodz Ghetto was the second largest.

**Litzmannstadt:** German name for the city of Lodz, in honour of German general Karl Litzmann who captured Lodz in World War I. The annexation of the city to Germany in November 1939 was intended to transform it into a predominantly German city, its Jewish inhabitants deported and its Polish residents thinned out. The Lodz Ghetto was intended as a short-term transit point, pending deportation.

**Lodz Ghetto:** A restricted area for Jews in the Baluty district of the Polish city Lodz; second largest ghetto in German-occupied Eastern Europe after the Warsaw Ghetto. The ghetto was sealed off on 1 May 1940, with a population of over 160,000 Jews. Initially intended as a temporary holding place for the Jews of Lodz until they could be deported, its organizational structure served as a model for the establishment of other ghettoes. It was the only ghetto in which smuggling was impossible because it was hermetically sealed. Most of the ghetto inhabitants worked as slave labourers in factories, primarily in the textile industry. The liquidation of the Lodz Ghetto began in the summer of 1944 with the deportation of many of its inhabitants to Chelmno or Auschwitz. The few who remained were liberated by the Soviet Red Army in January 1945. The Lodz Ghetto outlasted all other ghettoes in Eastern Europe.

**Medem, Vladimir:** (1879–1923) Popular Bundist leader. Born to assimilated Russian-Jewish parents in Minsk and baptized at birth in the Greek Orthodox Church, Medem developed a sense of Jewishness as a student at the University of Kiev in 1897, where he was exposed to Marxism and became acquainted with the Bund. Expelled from the university in 1899 for political activities, he joined the Bund. Arrested several times by Tsarist authorities, he resided in Warsaw from 1915 to 1920, joining the Central Committee of the Bund

**Mengele, Josef:** (1911–1979) Appointed SS garrison physician of Auschwitz in 1943, responsible for deciding which prisoners were fit for slave labour and which would be murdered immediately in the gas chambers; conducted sadistic experiments on Jewish and Roma prisoners.

**Morgenshtern:** A Bundist-affiliated sports club officially established in 1926, promoting physical education for Jewish workers and their children, especially through group activities such as gymnastics, hiking, and cycling, rather than competitive sports that emphasized individual accomplishments. In 1937, the Warsaw branch of Morgenshtern claimed to have 1500 active members, the largest local sports organization in of Poland.

**Peyes [Yiddish] / Peyot [Hebrew]:** Side-curls or earlocks. Among certain Orthodox Jewish communities, males refrain from cutting the hair at the edge of the face, in front of the ears. The practice of growing these distinctive locks of hair is based on a strict interpretation of the biblical verse "You shall not round off the side-growth [corners] of your head, or destroy the side-growth of your beard" (Lev. 19:27).

**Rumkowski, (Mordekhe) Chaim:** (1877-1944) Chief administrator of the Lodz Ghetto, appointed by the German authorities as head of the *Judenrat*, or Jewish Council, in charge of all Jewish public agencies and institutions in the ghetto, as well as the Jewish police. He served in this capacity from the ghetto's establishment until its liquidation in the summer of 1944, when he was deported to Auschwitz.

**SKIF:** [Yiddish] Acronym for *Sotsyalistisher kinder farbund*, or Socialist Children's Union; a Bundist-run children's organization in interwar Poland, offering after-school sports activities and educational lectures.

**SS:** Short for "Schutzstaffel," or Defense Corps, organized by Hitler in 1925 to protect him and other Nazi Party leaders. Under the directorship of Heinrich Himmler, the SS developed into an elite corps whose members were selected according to racial criteria. SS membership grew from 280 in 1929, to 50,000 when the Nazis came to power in 1933, to nearly a quarter of a million on the eve of World War II. In 1934, the SS assumed most police functions including the Gestapo, the secret state police. The SS administered the concentration camps, persecuted Jews, and suppressed political opponents through terror tactics.

**Zionism:** A Jewish national movement advocating the creation of a homeland for Jews in the Jewish historic homeland of the Land of Israel as a means to resolve the problem of persecution facing the Jews of Europe. Zionists promoted the revival of Hebrew as a Jewish national language. In interwar Poland, Zionism was one of many Jewish political parties with affiliated schools and youth groups.

INDEX

The Azrieli Foundation

The Azrieli Foundation was established in 1989 to realize and extend the philanthropic vision of David J. Azrieli, C.M., C.Q., MArch. The Foundation's mission is to support a wide spectrum of initiatives in education and research. The Azrieli Foundation is an active supporter of programs in the fields of Jewish education, the education of architects, scientific and medical research, and education in the arts. The Azrieli Foundation's many well-known initiatives include: the Holocaust Survivor Memoirs Publishing Program, which collects, preserves, publishes and distributes the written memoirs of survivors in Canada; the Azrieli Institute for Educational Empowerment, an innovative program successfully working to keep at-risk youth in school; and the Azrieli Fellows Program, which promotes academic excellence and leadership on the graduate level at Israeli universities. Programs sponsored and supported are located in Canada, Israel, and the United States.

YORK Centre for Jewish Studies at York University

In 1989, York University established Canada's first interdisciplinary research centre in Jewish studies. Over the years, the Centre for Jewish Studies at York (CJS) has earned national and international acclaim for its dynamic approach to teaching and research. While embracing Jewish culture and classical study in all its richness, the Centre also has a distinctly modern core, and a strong interest in the study of the Canadian Jewish experience.

York was the Canadian pioneer in the study of the Holocaust. The Centre maintains its strong commitment to the study of the Holocaust through the research, teaching, and community involvement of its faculty, its graduate diploma program in Advanced Hebrew and Jewish Studies, and its unique program — developed in cooperation with the Centre for German and European Studies — for Canadian, German and Polish education students.